PRAYERS
of a GOD
CHASER

Books by Tommy Tenney

TOMMY TENNEY

PRAYERS
of a GOD
CHASER

BETHANYHOUSE
MINNEAPOLIS, MINNESOTA

Published by Bethany House Publishers
A Ministry of Bethany Fellowship International
11400 Hampshire Avenue South
Bloomington, Minnesota 55438
www.bethanyhouse.com

Printed in the United States of America

Library of Congress Cataloging-in-Publication Data

Tenney, Tommy, 1956–
    Prayers of a God chaser : passionate prayers of pursuit / by Tommy Tenney.
        p. cm.
Includes bibliographical references.
    ISBN 0-7642-2734-3 (alk. paper)
    1. Prayer—Christianity. 2. God—Worship and love. I. Title.
BV220 .T46   2002
248.3'2—dc21
                                          2002010132

TOMMY TENNEY spent 10 years pastoring and has spent over 20 years in itinerant ministry, traveling to more than 40 nations. He speaks in over 150 venues each year sharing his heart with many thousands. His two passions are to seek the presence of God and encouraging unity in the body. To help others pursue these twin passions, he founded the GodChasers Network, a ministry organized to distribute his writing and speaking through various mediums. Tommy is a prolific author with more than one million books in print each year, and eight bestselling titles to date. His books have been translated into more than 30 languages.

Three generations of ministry in his family heritage have given Tommy a unique perspective on ministry. He has a gifting to lead hungry people into the presence of God. He and his wife, Jeannie, understand the value of intimacy with God and humility in serving God's people.

The Tenneys reside in Louisiana with their three daughters and two Yorkies.

DEDICATION

To hungry-hearted God Chasers everywhere,

to the countless volunteers and staff who have helped me fan

the flames of passion for God across the nation and the world, and

especially to the partners and supporters of the GodChasers Network

. . . may God answer your deepest heart's cry with

the wonder of His presence!

—Tommy Tenney

CONTENTS

FOREWORD

If you want to read a book that will help you drift off to sleep at night, then you don't want to read a Tommy Tenney book. His books have an energy that runs through them from the first page to the last. Before you even finish the second paragraph, you are swept up by his gut-level honesty, refreshing clarity, and passion for the presence of God, and he doesn't let you down until after you have finished the final sentence. Before you know it, you are up praying. Forget falling asleep.

In this book, Tommy tells us that the pursuit of God's presence comes with a price, as does anything of great value. When we are willing to pay whatever it is, we win. In other words, if we *want* all God *has*, then we have to *give* all God *wants*. And God wants many different kinds of prayer. Tommy takes us through each kind—prayers of intercession, repentance, guidance, surrender, commitment, pursuit, faith, and struggle, to name a few—with examples of each from Scripture. This opens up our vision so we can get beyond praying for what we need, which we *should do*, to praying for what God wants, which we *must do*.

I love to pray, and I pray a lot, but reading this book inspires me to pray more. It makes me long for the fullness of God's presence. It makes me realize what a waste of time my prayerless days have been.

I am often asked, "What made you become an expert on prayer?" My answer is always the same: "Desperation!"

I'm no expert on anything. But I have been desperate all my life. Before I knew the Lord, I was desperate for anything that would take my pain away. After I came to know the Lord, I was desperate for answers to my prayers. Now I'm desperate for more of God. I want to know Him better and experience Him more fully. And this book by Tommy Tenney confirms what I have felt all along: Desperation can be an admirable trait if what you are desperate for is more of the Lord. And prayer that comes from the desperation of our hearts carries with it the fervency God loves.

In the times we live in, we cannot afford to have a passionless or lukewarm relationship with God. We must know Him intimately and hear Him absolutely. We need to walk so closely with God that He can lift us above our limitations and transform us. We have to live in Him and remain in Him. We can't only *think* we have the power of God flowing through us; we have to experience it. When we experience it, we have an encounter with God that changes our lives forever. Who among us doesn't need that?

—Stormie Omartian

CHAPTER 1

PRAYERS

of A GOD CHASER

W hat is prayer?

When I started writing this book, I believed I was writing a book about prayer. I plunged into the theology of prayer and began to research the subject with stacks of books new and old. Then I realized God hadn't commissioned me to write an anthology of prayer.

Theological scholars and church leaders far wiser than I have categorized and subdivided the spiritual act of prayer into an incredible variety of forms, types, and methodologies.

Mine is a much humbler goal: to share the prayers and principles of prayer that energized, transformed, and revolutionized my life, my relationship with God, and everything I thought I knew about ministry.

I still remember when the first flickering prayer flame sprang to life in me. I was sixteen and had casually pulled a book from the shelf of my dad's library. (More because it had a "cool" cover than for any other reason.) It was Leonard Ravenhill's book on prayer, *Why Revival Tarries*. I can still quote it:

The Cinderella of the church of today is the prayer meeting. This handmaid of the Lord is unloved and unwooed because she is not dripping with the pearls of intellectualism, nor glamorous with the silks of philosophy; neither is she enchanting with the tiara of psychology. She wears the homespuns of sincerity and humility and so is not afraid to kneel!

The offense of prayer is that it does not essentially tie in to mental efficiency. (That is not to say that prayer is a partner to mental sloth; in these days efficiency is at a premium.) Prayer is conditioned by one thing alone and that is spirituality. One does not need to be spiritual to preach, that is, to make and deliver sermons of homiletical perfection and exegetical exactitude. By a combination of memory, knowledge, ambition, personality, plus well-lined bookshelves, self-confidence and a sense of having arrived—brother, the pulpit is yours almost anywhere these days. Preaching of the type mentioned affects men; prayer affects God. Preaching affects time; prayer affects eternity. The pulpit can be a shop window to display our talents; the closet speaks death to display.[1]

I also have some favorite prayers in the Bible that have greatly affected me: Moses' prayer to see God's glory, Elijah's pointed and powerful prayers, David's passionate pursuit of the presence of God and his heartbroken plea to "be back where I was with you" before the sin with Bathsheba.

All of these are verbal voicings eager for encounters, but some of the greatest prayers were "unspoken." I remember growing up hearing pastors in church services ask, "Are there any unspoken requests?"

John leaning on Jesus' breast was prayer, a silent plea for intimacy. Often, when my children come into my arms, they cannot express how they feel. Prayer can be as simple as curling up in a ball and hearing God say, "I know what you need."

One of my favorite authors, Richard Foster, subdivided prayer into twenty-one categories with excellent explanations and examples for each one in a book entitled *Prayer: Finding the Heart's True Home.*[2] This is just one of many excellent books I recommend to "God Chasers" who want to "plumb the depths" of prayer in their pursuit of God's presence. Richard Foster, a Quaker who serves as the Jack and Barbara Lee Distinguished Professor of Spiritual Formation at Azusa Pacific University, lists his twenty-one categories of prayer as follows: Simple Prayer, Prayer of the Forsaken, The Prayer of Examen [examination], The Prayer of Tears, The Prayer of Relinquishment, Formation Prayer, Covenant Prayer, The Prayer of Adoration, The Prayer of Rest, Sacramental Prayer, Unceasing Prayer, The Prayer of the Heart, Meditative Prayer, Contemplative Prayer, Praying the Ordinary, Petitionary Prayer, Intercessory Prayer, Healing Prayer, The Prayer of Suffering, Authoritative Prayer, and Radical Prayer. But the most common approach to describing prayer follows a simpler path and views it through seven simple categories based on the seven segments of The Lord's Prayer.[3]

Jesus simplified things even further and divided prayer into two categories when He said, "Two men went up to the temple to pray, one a Pharisee and the other a tax collector."[4] He described the first prayer category this way: "The Pharisee stood and prayed thus *with himself.*"[5]

The Lord went on to describe the content of the man's prayer in detail, but the most significant thing I noticed about the Pharisee's prayer is that he prayed *with himself.* His "audience of one" didn't seem to include God as a major participant. (It seems God wasn't really interested in joining *that* private prayer meeting!)

The second category of prayer was epitomized by someone far less prestigious, powerful, and respected than the Pharisee. He was a sinner, and he had sense enough to know it. In his desperation, humility, and hunger for God, he prayed a prayer that was totally different from that of the politically correct petitioner.

I suspect that many modern readers unconsciously discount the second man's prayer because it was punctuated by embarrassingly passionate episodes of chest pounding and desperate cries of repentance. (Perhaps modern "passion police" would have been on him in a split second for disturbing our church services!)[6]

Perhaps you've noticed the dulling glaze that seems to settle over the faces of most churchgoers when someone introduces the subject of prayer from the pulpit or during a dinner conversation. Why does this happen? We think prayer is boring, because we think of it as hard work done in secret with few if any results.

The only time we perk up is when a gifted orator steps forward to entertain us with a flowery "performance" prayer in public. There is nothing wrong with public prayers—God just seems to dislike "professional prayers." He prefers "passionate prayers."

> God just seems to dislike "professional prayers." He prefers "passionate prayers."

The church faces a serious problem today because Jesus said the

Father hears and answers the prayers of desperate sinners and passionate saints, but He seemingly ignores the fancy prayers of the pompous and the religiously correct.

What kinds of prayers fill your church services, prayer meetings, and private devotions? Is God drawn to the passion of your pursuit? Is He distracted by your desire and attracted to the desperate hunger of your longing for your first love?[7]

Most of us find it hard to pray at times (if not *most* of the time), and I confess I have far to go and much to learn as a God Chaser and as a man of prayer. While working on this book I discovered another "brother of the heart" in a campus minister and author named Ben Patterson, who wrote:

> I'm not "into" prayer. I seem to have missed the religious gene or whatever it is that makes people enjoy the act of praying. It's not my nature to pray. *I'm not into prayer, I am into God!* I thirst and hunger for God, I ache for God. Without His everlasting arms holding me up, I will fall. So I must pray.[8]

I don't claim to have climbed the Mount Everest of prayer, but I am still inspired by its summit. I've walked with God since my boyhood and have served as a minister of the Gospel since my teens, but I still long for more intimate moments in His presence.

To tell you the truth, some of my greatest encounters with God occurred in places far away from stained-glass windows, carpeted worship facilities, or exciting Christian gatherings.

With the hectic schedule I keep in the ministry, I openly confess that my best "prayer closet" is in the shower (cell phones and pagers are the bane of intimacy with a spouse or with God). The shower stall seems to be my primary place of refuge. (When God is speaking, I've been known to take as many as three showers a day!) Perhaps I need to install a kneeler—and some stained glass!

God often prefers to meet us at the point of our desperation, our passion, and our hunger. He finds that ground more sacred than our monuments to accomplishments and self-reliance.

I want to inspire you to desire to pray, and also provide you a resource to *help* you pray. Sometimes you may have to do as King Hezekiah did when he spread out a letter in the temple. Spread out this book in your prayer closet. Perhaps the prayers offered here will help you pray and teach you until you can fly on your own. You can't do it by praying my prayers, but you can use patterns of prayer to create your own prayers.

> God often prefers to meet us at the point of our desperation, our passion, and our hunger.

Some may view any reference to weapons or violence as politically incorrect, but the apostle Paul also lived in a violent era and he viewed things differently. Although he did not advocate spiritual violence, he had no problem describing our "mighty" weaponry of spiritual warfare or advocating their diligent use.[9]

In the natural realm, we understand the sorrow created when the forces of evil bring death and injury to innocent victims. However, prayer is our primary weapon, providing the ability to slip incognito behind the lines of the forces of darkness and destroy the works of our spiritual foes and their human agents.[10]

In the natural realm, the power of a crooked finger on a slender piece of metal is trivial except when that piece of metal is the trigger of a loaded gun!

In the spiritual realm, your voice and heart lifted in prayer is the "trigger." God's Word and will are the explosive charge. His divine answer is the bullet of inescapable change speeding toward its divinely inspired target. Ready. Aim. *Pray!*

PRAYERS *of* DESPERATION

In the agonizing moments just before Jesus Christ crossed the line from life to death, the Son of God cried out in the only language passionate enough for such a heartrending crisis: He released His pain in the dialect of desperation. Only moments later He whispered something all creation waited to hear: "It is finished!"[1]

Desperation has been a doorway to divine encounter for virtually everyone who calls upon the name of the Lord. None of us will ever carry the load of sorrow Jesus bore that long night in Gethsemane or upon the cross at Golgotha, but most of us have tasted the pain of desperation nonetheless.

I know it wasn't my polished prayers as a professional preacher or pastor that brought me to an encounter with God years ago. My perfected phrases of King James prose didn't bring me heart to heart with the heavenly Father—He met me in the midst of my inarticulate and passionate pleas of desperation and tears of frustration.

I was a born-again, third-generation preacher who loved God; but a holy desperation had seized my soul. I knew the traditions of religion could no longer satisfy me. I tried to describe the heart hunger I felt in *The God Chasers*. I portrayed the persistent ache that wouldn't go away as a "gnawing vacuum of emptiness in the midst of my accomplishments" and "a divine desperation of destiny."[2]

It took nothing less than a divine encounter to satisfy my soul's awakened and uncontrollable appetite for God's presence. When it finally came, I knew I would never be the same.

When I think of Jesus' desperate cry to His Father from the cross, it seems to me His greatest challenge wasn't the choking burden of humanity's sin that enveloped Him like an unwanted mantle of contamination. It was the *unbearable separation* from the Father, whom He had known and communed with since before the creation of the universe.

THE AGONY OF SEPARATION
BIRTHS DESPERATION

Jesus had never known the desperation of such separation.[3] It is no surprise that desperation in the human heart is usually rooted in the agony of separation from God and from destiny, the death of a dream, the loss of a loved one, or separation from hope itself.

Some may wonder why I am so interested in prayer, since worship seems to play such a prominent place in so many of my books. Worship

> Worship
> *is*
> prayer.

is prayer. I've found that the intimacy with God we encounter in true worship actually produces a greater appreciation for prayer in all of its forms (much as it produces a greater love and passion for the lost).

E. M. Bounds said it this way when talking about the prayer life of Moses:

Intimate as he was with God, his intimacy did not abate the necessity of prayer. This intimacy only brought clearer insight into the nature and necessity of prayer, and led him to see the greater obligations to pray and to discover the larger results of praying. In reviewing one of the crises through which Israel passed, when the very existence of the nation was in peril, he writes: "I fell down before the Lord forty days and forty nights." *Wonderful praying and wonderful results! Moses knew how to do wonderful praying, and God knew how to give wonderful results.*[4]

The desperate prayer of a barren woman in the Old Testament survived the ravages of more than three thousand years of human history and dilution to become a model of the power released through the prayer of desperation. (We can still learn much from the prayers of those who have gone before us.)[5]

RAW DESPERATION IGNORES RELIGIOUS DISAPPROVAL

The Bible describes the day Hannah cried out to God for a child in unedited and raw desperation while a religious leader eavesdropped in open disapproval:

> And [Hannah] was in bitterness of soul, and prayed to the Lord and wept in anguish. Then she made a vow and said, "O Lord of hosts, if You will indeed look on the affliction of Your maidservant and remember me, and not forget Your maidservant, but will give Your maidservant a male child, then I will give him to the Lord all the days of his life, and no razor shall come upon his head."[6]

Eli the priest had grown comfortable with the predictable; he assumed God was pleased with passionless expressions of devotion and petition. When the priest saw Hannah sobbing and mouthing silent words near the door of the tabernacle, he saw only uncontrolled emotion probably promoted by alcohol and human excess displayed in an inappropriate place.

God saw things differently. This was the defining moment of passionate prayer that would birth a prophet/priest named Samuel who would one day anoint another prophet, priest, and king named David.

Prayers of desperation rarely spring from moments of joy or deep satisfaction. They are conceived in crisis, gestated in the gruesome grind of life, and birthed in turmoil and pain.

GOD'S MEGAPHONE TO A DEAF WORLD

It almost seems that the Divine Object of our passion personally creates urgency in our hearts birthed in the midst of our chaos and pain. C. S. Lewis said, "God whispers to us in our pleasures, speaks to us in our consciences, but shouts to us in our pains: it is his megaphone to rouse a deaf world."[7]

> If desperation has seized your soul, perhaps it is time to release it all in a desperate prayer to the Lover of your soul.

If desperation has seized your soul in the form of hunger, fear, weakness, spiritual thirst, or despair, perhaps it is time to release it all in a desperate prayer to the Lover of your soul. He is your hope, your song, and your Deliverer. He has never stopped loving you, and He never will. He is waiting. . . .

In the early days of the revival movement in Great Britain's Hebrides Islands, Duncan Campbell had just closed a service and noticed the people seemed reluctant to leave. Then when most of the people had left the church building, a desperate young man stood and prayed.

According to Duncan Campbell: "This young man stood up. I'll never forget the words he said: 'Oh God, *You promised!*' All of a sudden it sounded like chariot wheels were rumbling on the roof of the church building. The next thing we knew, the church was filling up again!"[8] *This is the prayer of desperation inspired and empowered by the Holy Spirit.*

E. M. Bounds said this about the need for desperate prayer:

> The soldiers in the warfare against the Devil must understand how to wear the armor of *"all prayer."* The demand is for *"all prayer"* at all seasons, in the [most] intense form, with a deep sense of personal need for God. Prayer must deepen and intensify into supplication. The Holy Spirit will help us into this kind of mighty praying and clothe us with this irresistible power of prayer.[9]

Too many of us land in the pit of desperation through our own procrastination. Even worse, many of us live more like Jonah than Jesus, and we wonder why we wake up one day in the belly of our own disobedience. Some of us even have the audacity to blame God for our fall and complain because He hasn't delivered us from our self-made dilemmas.

Jonah's problems began the day he decided to run from God's will. When he finally grew tired of wallowing in the digestive juices of his seagoing home (it doesn't matter whether it was a big fish or a whale— neither "model" could have been pleasant), he prayed the wrong prayer at the wrong time:

"God, I want *out* of the belly of this beast!"

God's answer displayed Deity's usual preoccupation with where we should *be* (for some reason we are preoccupied with where we should *not* be). God said in effect, "Jonah, I want you *in* Nineveh!" Once the errant prophet agreed to go where God wanted him to go, he found himself beached on dry land within walking distance of Nineveh with a second opportunity to obey.

OVERCOME EVERY OBJECTION AND OBSTACLE TO PRAYER

Refuse to surrender to the Enemy's distractions and deterrents to prayer. John C. Maxwell, a respected speaker, made five simple recommendations that may help you overcome the usual objections and obstacles to prayer:[10]

1. Be spontaneous.
2. Be specific.
3. ASK the right way (*A*sk with pure motives, *S*eek with effort, *K*nock persistently).
4. Pray with all your heart (pray aloud, write down the distractions—the prayer requests that come throughout the day, keep a prayer journal).
5. Pray continually.

Jesus knew where He was supposed to be, and He openly acknowledged the reluctance of His flesh to go to the grave, yet He did it anyway. He embraced His destiny after He overcame His fears, pain, and the uncertainty of His flesh (after all, God had never experienced death in any form until God's Son gave up the ghost on the cross at Calvary).

DESPERATE PRAYER AND THE HEART OF REVIVAL

There is another prayer of desperation that seems to embody the heart of revival in this generation. It is the cry of blind Bartimaeus to Jesus from his place in the dust and dregs of society from the side of life's road: "Jesus, Son of David, have mercy on me!"[11]

Once again, I want to tap the prayer-birthed writings of E. M. Bounds to summarize the power and biblical purpose of desperate prayer:

> Prayer is not acting a part or going through religious motions. Prayer is neither official nor formal nor ceremonial, but direct, hearty, intense. The object of asking is to receive. The aim of seeking is to find. The purpose of knocking is to arouse attention and get in.[12]

This generation desperately needs revival, but revival must begin with us. Only the passionate and the inspired dare to become carriers of God's fire. One early church Father wrote,

It's time to arrest heaven's attention!

> Let us stretch our minds toward heaven. Held fast by that desire, we seek to be absorbed and immersed by spiritual fire. *Anyone filled with the fire of inspiration has no fear of anyone, whether wild beast or man. Armed with fire,*

this person does not fear traps because he knows danger retreats as he approaches. *Such fire cannot be withstood or endured because it is all-consuming.*[13]

So much for ceremony and official formalities. It's time to arrest heaven's attention! If you are desperate, He is close! Pray this prayer with all the passion God has planted in your heart:

≡≡≡

PRAYER OF DESPERATION

Lord Jesus, my soul aches at the mere mention of Your name. My heart leaps for every rumor of Your coming, and each possibility that You will manifest Your presence. I'm not satisfied with mere spiritual dainties. I'm ravenously hungry for You in your fullness. I'm desperate to feast on the bread of Your presence and quench my thirst with the wine of Your Spirit.[14]

CHAPTER 3

PRAYERS
of REPENTANCE

HAVE MERCY UPON ME, O GOD, ACCORDING

TO YOUR LOVINGKINDNESS; ACCORDING TO

THE MULTITUDE OF YOUR TENDER MERCIES,

BLOT OUT MY TRANSGRESSIONS. WASH ME

THOROUGHLY FROM MY INIQUITY, AND

CLEANSE ME FROM MY SIN. FOR I

ACKNOWLEDGE MY TRANSGRESSIONS, AND

MY SIN IS ALWAYS BEFORE ME.

PSALM 51:1-3

The man who wrote the above fervent prayer for forgiveness discovered he had impregnated a married woman; then he planned and
implemented the murder of the woman's husband.

To add insult to fatal injury, the murder victim was a soldier and
officer who was totally loyal to his murderer (who also happened to be
the man's king and commanding officer). This schemer even had the

intended victim unknowingly deliver sealed instructions concerning his own murder to a field commander who obediently carried out the king's scheme.[1]

The Machiavellian murderer seeking forgiveness was also a nationally respected spiritual leader and the author of the most celebrated praise and worship songs in history. He prayed this prayer in tears, knowing his life, his kingdom, his ministry, and the multigenerational covenant God had made with him were all on the line.

This prayer is especially important to me because this "sorry excuse for a man" was none other than King David the psalmist and one of the greatest God-Chasing worshipers the world has ever known.

Does it seem plausible that we are talking about the youthful worshiper/warrior who single-handedly defeated Goliath and later became Israel's greatest king?

How can this "woman chaser" be restored and rehabilitated to become a God Chaser? What kind of prayer do you pray to be forgiven this magnitude of debauchery?

HIS KEY TO GREATNESS: HIS ABILITY TO ACCESS GRACE

How could this murderer and adulterer be the biblical predecessor of the Messiah? Only by the mercy and grace of God offered in response to *true repentance.* Wisdom and personal charisma were *not* the keys to King David's greatness—*it was his ability to access grace.* This is the raw power of the prayer of repentance.

David had as many if not more faults than contemporary readers, yet God said of him, "I have found David the son of Jesse, *a man after My own heart, who will do all My will.* From this man's seed, according to the promise, God raised up for Israel a Savior; Jesus."[2]

The passionate prayer of repentance is important because repentance is the New Testament equivalent of Old Testament sackcloth and ashes and blood sacrifice. The prayer of repentance is the key ingredient in the recipe for restoration.

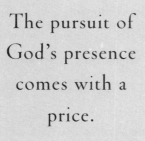

The pursuit of God's presence comes with a price.

Repentance is required of anyone who wants to encounter the presence of God and live. "The Aaronic priest knew something about God that we need to rediscover today. They knew that God is holy, and mankind is not. They knew that living flesh would instantly die if it encountered the unshielded, uncovered glory of God."[3]

Under the old covenant, God wanted to come close to mankind, but He knew His holiness would destroy any living flesh because of the contaminating sin it carried. It took an elaborate covering of blood, the smoke of incense, and holy garments to keep a priest alive for only a few minutes in God's manifest presence behind the veil.

He still says to those who would draw close, "Be careful; be careful. If you're going to get any closer, then make sure everything is dead. If you really want to know Me, everything [in you] must die."[4] Paul the apostle said, "No flesh should glory in His presence."[5] Repentance is flesh-death in order to bring about spirit-life!

If you claim to be one of God's own, then you had better become intimately acquainted with the passionate prayer of repentance, because you will need it. The pursuit of God's presence comes with a price.

REPENTANCE PUTS OFFENSE TO DEATH

As humans, we are prone to weakness and failure. Why does it seem easier to grow weeds than it is to grow crops? Every small annoyance and confrontation with other people—including people in the church—may create an offense and contaminate our hearts, unless repentance puts it to death.[6]

Patrick D. Miller, professor of Old Testament theology at Princeton University, mentioned something that should chill the heart of every true believer and drive us even faster to our knees in times of sin and trespass. Miller was writing about David's confession of sin with Bathsheba when he said:

> The sin against the brother or sister is viewed as sin against the Lord and an occasion for confession before God and the seeking of divine forgiveness. Such a confession warns against an *easy division of the commandments* into those that have to do with God and those that have to do with the neighbor.[7]

If you've done it to them, you've done it to Him! If you hope to passion-ately pursue God and abide in His presence, be prepared to pursue holi-ness and purity in your life and in your relationships with others. Jesus requires no less than this.

As I wrote in *The God Chasers*:

> We don't understand the delicate matter of approaching the glory of God today. We talk about the glory and say, "The glory is here," but it really isn't. The anointing is here, and there may be a measure of the light of God. But if the glory of God ever showed up in full measure, we'd all be dead. Mountains melt at His manifest presence; how much more man's flesh!
>
> . . . If there is flesh present when the glory of God comes, then it will have to be dead flesh, because nothing can live in that pres-ence. The only mortal thing that can remain in His manifest pres-ence and stand is "dead" flesh, because only dead men can see His face.[8]

MURDERERS STILL PRAY
THIS PRAYER

Mercy-seeking men and women still pray this prayer of repentance penned by King David. Murderers still come to God with these words bathed in tears and remorse, and I suspect that many of their victims' families also use this prayer to approach God's throne for mercy and grace and to overcome their anger and hatred of the murderer.

Adulterers still fall on their faces with the words of David's repentant prayer on their lips, seeking the strength to break off their sinful liaison and for mercy to walk holy before God once again. But sensuous adulterers have no more need for prayers of repentance than those with sour attitudes. The prayer of repentance is not just needed for the *big* sins. It must become a lifestyle of walking in verbalized forgiveness.

Preachers, prostitutes, and college professors in the grip of godly conviction still turn to David's ancient prayer of death to self and sin, hoping to get right with God once again. Why? *Repentance is God's key to the door of supernatural restoration.*

REPENTANCE IS THE NEW TESTAMENT EQUIVALENT OF DEATH

The days of blood sacrifices and the Old Testament priestly ordinances are gone because Jesus Christ, our High Priest and the sacrificed Lamb of God, took upon himself the full load of our sin and failure. The key to all under the new covenant is *repentance.* "That is why repentance and brokenness—*the New Testament equivalent of death*—brings the manifest presence of God so near."[9]

Some people continue to have a serious problem with my use of the word *passionate.* Why must prayers of repentance be passionate? Let me answer the question with a question: *Just how legitimate is any act of repentance or request for forgiveness without passion of some kind?*

The act of repentance is not a performance or mere mental exercise—it *must* come from the heart filled with godly sorrow over sin if it is ever to be heard, received, and granted by God.

The apostle Paul gave us what must be one of the most compact and powerful pictures of the true work (and prayer) of repentance:

> Now I rejoice, not that you were made sorry, but that your sorrow led to repentance. For you were made sorry in a godly manner, that you might suffer loss from us in nothing.
>
> *For godly sorrow produces repentance leading to salvation,* not to be regretted; but the sorrow of the world produces death.
>
> For observe this very thing, that you sorrowed in a godly manner: What *diligence* it produced in you, what *clearing of yourselves,* what *indignation,* what *fear,* what *vehement desire,* what *zeal,* what *vindication!* In all things you proved yourselves to be clear in this matter.[10]

When Jesus compared the prayers of the pompous Pharisee and the passionate and penitent publican (or tax collector), He was measuring more than the simple text of their prayers. I'm convinced that He was also weighing the motivation and passion of the heart and the genuine sincerity of their prayers.

The words of the Pharisee were birthed in a heart filled with pride, spiritual arrogance, and hypocrisy. The pleas of the publican were birthed in the anguish of true brokenhearted repentance, and Jesus confirmed that his passionate prayer was instantly answered.[11] Pharisaical praying proves you can say the right mantra with a wrong motive. Man may call that "praying," but I'm not sure God does.

DO YOU PRAY
LIKE A PERFORMING PHARISEE
OR A PLEADING PUBLICAN?

If you were to qualify your more recent prayers of repentance, would you be forced to admit that the "quickie nighttime prayer" you rattled off five minutes before you fell asleep was more like the Pharisee's perform-ance? Or would you wipe away tears of joy as you remembered the divine encounter you experienced after pouring out your heart to God in bro-kenness and repentance yesterday? It isn't the formula that counts, nor is it measured simply by the "drama" of your delivery. Prayer begins in the heart and is launched on the passion and fervency of your cries to God.

Genuine disciples of Jesus Christ rarely need encouragement to repent. They have learned early in their walk that it pays rich dividends to "live clean" before God by practicing a life-style of repentance. God seemingly asked us to do the impossible when He said in His Word: "But as He who called you is holy, you also be holy in all your conduct, because it is written, '*Be holy, for I am holy.*'"[12]

> Genuine disciples of Jesus Christ rarely need encouragement to repent.

Yet He also provided the perfect Helper when He sent the Holy Spirit to dwell in our hearts.[13] It is the God who dwells within you who empowers you to live a lifestyle of repentance and to "live holy." It seems

I remember reading somewhere, "For it is God who works in you both to will and to do for His good pleasure."[14]

GREAT LEADERS AND GOD CHASERS BECOME GREAT REPENTERS

Sin, failure, resentments, hurts, and unresolved issues come up in our lives even when we face no real obstacle or demonic opposition. Yet everything seems to intensify when a follower of Christ decides to step up the pace of their pursuit of Him. Great leaders—and great God Chasers—face great challenges, and many of the greatest pioneers in the church were forced to become "great repenters" as well. It is necessary when you make up your mind to live holy before a holy God.

God used John Wesley to help ignite revival on two continents in the late 1700s, and Wesley wrote a powerful prayer for forgiveness that has been offered to God on many lips in many different generations since that day. It is our turn today to pray his prayer of repentance:

═══

PLEA FOR FORGIVENESS

Forgive them all, O Lord:
our sins of omission and our sins of commission;

the sins of our youth and the sins of our riper years;

the sins of our souls and the sins of our bodies;

our secret and our more open sins;

our sins of ignorance and surprise;

and our more deliberate and presumptuous sin;

the sins we have done to please ourselves

and the sins we have done to please others;

the sins we know and remember,

and the sins we have forgotten;

the sins we have striven to hide from others

and the sins by which we have made others offend;

forgive them, O Lord, forgive them all for his sake,

who died for our sins and rose for our justification,

and now stands at thy right hand to make intercession for

us, Jesus Christ our Lord.[15]

CHAPTER 4

PRAYERS
of A HUNGRY HEART

═══

AS THE DEER PANTS FOR THE WATER BROOKS,

SO PANTS MY SOUL FOR YOU, O GOD.

MY SOUL THIRSTS FOR GOD, FOR THE

LIVING GOD.

WHEN SHALL I COME AND APPEAR

BEFORE GOD?

MY TEARS HAVE BEEN MY FOOD DAY

AND NIGHT,

WHILE THEY CONTINUALLY SAY TO ME,

"WHERE IS YOUR GOD?"

WHEN I REMEMBER THESE THINGS,

I POUR OUT MY SOUL WITHIN ME.

PSALM 42:1–4

═══

It seems to me that God intentionally launched King David beyond the time barrier and into the future as a worship pioneer. Somehow he managed to set a standard of worship we are still striving to match.

David went places in the spirit that we still struggle to find and enter. This man so passionately loved and longed for God *before the birth of Christ and the finished work of the cross* that his holy heartache still moves and motivates us today, thousands of years after his death.

We don't really have to theorize on the possibility—God prophesied it as part of His divine purpose in the earth:

> After this I will return and will *rebuild the tabernacle of David,* which has fallen down; I will rebuild its ruins, and I will set it up; so that the rest of mankind may seek the Lord, even all the Gentiles who are called by My name, says the Lord who does all these things.[1]

TASTE AND SEE—THE DIVINE GATEWAY TO HOLY ADDICTION

Hunger is a strange condition. When hunger is satisfied, it always seems to return later in even greater strength. This is especially true of hunger for God's presence—the *one true addiction* of the human soul and the only vital life source He created us to crave. Perhaps this is why the Scriptures say, "Oh, taste and see that the Lord is good."[2]

This verse marks the divine gateway to holy addiction and godward obsession. The more you stoke the flames of passion for Him, the more passionately hungry you get.

On the other hand, unsatisfied hunger rages at first but then grows fatally weak and compliant. Those who enter a forty-day fast will tell you that the first three to five days are extremely difficult. After that the hunger pangs subside, and a dulling listlessness sets in that becomes more prominent toward the end of the fast. The human body modifies its metabolism to survive on fewer and fewer nutrients, sapping its internal stores of fat, carbohydrates, and protein until it starts robbing living tissues just to keep the body alive.

Former First Lady Eleanor Roosevelt carried a prayer in her Bible that seemed to prescribe a divine cure or preventive for spiritual listlessness for those with courage to pray it in faith: *Our Father, who has set a restlessness in our hearts and made us all seekers after that which we can never fully find . . . keep us at tasks too hard for us, that we may be driven to Thee for strength.*[3]

God deliver us from this listless loss of appetite for the holy. Sometimes I fear the church has spiritual anorexia, or worse. We've grown content to subsist on empty calories or to simply "show up" at the Lord's dinner table but never eat. We are too busy talking about ourselves and criticizing the appearance and actions of others to stoke the flames of our spiritual hunger.

HOW DO YOU ORCHESTRATE CORPORATE HUNGER?

This takes us back to David and his simplified tabernacle. His raw hunger for God's presence signaled the return of divine glory to Jerusalem. King David's ability to orchestrate *corporate hunger* in the form of continual worship and prayer in that unwalled tabernacle or tent *kept* the glory there, and it also kept the people hungry for more of God. As I said in *God's Favorite House*:

> Nothing separated mankind from God's blue flame [signifying His presence] in David's house. In fact, *the only thing encircling God's presence in David's tabernacle were the worshipers* who ministered to Him 24 hours a day, 7 days a week, 365 days a year for an estimated 36 years! . . . In David's tabernacle the glory of God was seen by everyone—whether they were worshipers, passersby, or heathen. *Unveiled worship created unhindered view!*
>
> The miracle of "God's favorite house" can be traced to David's desire [hunger] *for God's presence.*[4]

I suspect there are many keys to remaining hungry, but one of them is to focus on the presence of God more than on the blessings and empowerments of God.

HUNGER PLAYS A KEY ROLE IN EFFECTIVE PRAYER

Ben Patterson understood the role of hunger in effective prayer when he wrote:

> Since the best teacher of prayer is the Holy Spirit, the best way to learn to pray is by praying. Whether, and how much we pray is, I think, finally *a matter of appetite, of hunger for God* and all that he is and desires.
>
> C. S. Lewis wrote in *The Weight of Glory*: "We are far too easily

pleased." That, in the end, is the reason we do not pray more than we do. Nothing less than infinite joy is offered us in God's kingdom of light. He has promised that we will one day shine like the sun in that kingdom (Matthew 13:43).

We have become satisfied with mere church, mere religious exertion, mere numbers and buildings—the things we can do. There is nothing wrong with these things, but they are no more than foam left by the surf on the ocean of God's glory and goodness.[5]

MOSES WAS SO HUNGRY HE WAITED FIFTEEN HUNDRED YEARS FOR THE DIVINE ENCOUNTER

Moses seemed to have everything in his life and ministry. God used him to humble the world's most powerful and dominant nation, while delivering his own people to freedom. He enjoyed an intimacy with God unequaled in many respects, and he walked in great spiritual authority—*yet he hungered for more.* He was so hungry that he waited fifteen hundred years for what he longed for—to see the face of God. This man's desperate prayer of hunger for God has been burned into my own heart:

And he said, "*Please, show me Your glory.*" Then He said, "I will make all My goodness pass before you, and I will proclaim the name of the Lord before you. I will be gracious to whom I will be gracious, and I will have compassion on whom I will have compassion." *But He said, "You cannot see My face; for no man shall see Me, and live."*[6]

What does this Old Testament passage say to us today? "Why would we need to pay attention to this conversation?" some would say. "Aren't we under the new covenant?" The Bible is the Word of God from front cover to back cover. As for this passage, it says a lot to us about hunger and prayer. I once wrote:

> When Moses told God, "Show me Your glory," the Lord said, "You can't, Moses. Only dead men can see My face." Fortunately Moses didn't stop there. Unfortunately, the Church did.
>
> It would have been easy for this man to be satisfied with God's first answer, but he wasn't. Moses wasn't selfish or presumptuous. He wasn't seeking material things or personal fame. He wasn't even seeking miracles or gifts. . . . Moses simply wanted *God*, and that is the greatest gift and blessing we can ever give Him. Yet Moses had to *pursue* Him, and it didn't come easy.[7]

HE CHOSE INTIMACY OVER POWER

Moses, the great leader who defied Pharaoh and led the Israelites across the dry bed of the Red Sea and through the wilderness, wanted more than the gifts and provision of God's hands. *He chose intimacy over power.* We should adopt Moses' standard as our own. In essence, he was saying, "God, I want to see you with your hair down . . . with your glory unraveled. . . ." *Which would you choose?* "I don't want to see Your 'acts'— I want to see Your face!"

Sometimes the prayer of the hungry heart takes the form of action or reveals its power through hot tears and the silence of brokenness. It is a mistake to assume that the passionate prayer of hunger is synonymous with loud prayer.

> Sometimes the prayer of the hungry heart reveals its power through hot tears and the silence of brokenness.

One of the "loudest" of these silent action prayers ever offered to God happened in an unlikely place at an unlikely time with the most unlikely person conceivable at that time.

> Then one of the Pharisees asked Him to eat with him. And He went to the Pharisee's house, and sat down to eat. And behold, a woman in the city who was a sinner, when she knew that Jesus sat at the table in the Pharisee's house, brought an alabaster flask of fragrant oil, and stood at His feet behind Him weeping; and she began to wash His feet with her tears, and wiped them with the hair of her head; and she kissed His feet and anointed them with the fragrant oil.[8]

This "sinful woman" expressed her reverent love for the Lord more skillfully, purely, and "loudly" than anyone else in the room, including the highly educated Pharisee host and twelve handpicked disciples of Jesus.

SOME CALLED IT A "WASTE," BUT JESUS CALLED IT WORSHIP

"*The disciples were so embarrassed by the woman's actions that they wanted to throw her out*, but Jesus made her actions an eternal monument of selfless worship!"[9] The disciples called her extravagant gift of oil in the alabaster box a "waste," but Jesus called it *worship*—and she never said a word.

Another common misunderstanding about the prayer of the hungry heart is that it always involves *many words over much time*. Yitzhak Buxbaum, a noted Jewish authority on the fervent prayer of Hasidic Jewish worshipers, said:

> A famous story says the Baal Shem Tov [the founder of Hasidism, a pietistic, mystic branch of Judaism originating in the eighteenth century] once stopped at the door of a synagogue, saying he could not enter because it was so full of prayers. When his astonished disciples asked him if that was not the best recommendation for a synagogue, he answered that when prayers are said with sincerity, they ascend to heaven—but here, since they were said by rote, they did not ascend and entirely filled the synagogue; there was no room for him to enter![10]

GOD'S HUNGER RESPONDS TO YOUR HUNGER

I wonder if perhaps God faces the same problem when He tries to enter some of our services? Avoid "religion by rote." (Rituals are not necessarily "rote," for God has responded to the passionate hunger expressed by sincere worshipers through ritual for many centuries.) Remember that God's hunger for worship responds to your hunger.

Here is some invaluable advice on prayer that may be of great help in your passionate pursuit of God's presence:

> Tell God all that is in your heart, as one unloads one's heart to a dear friend. People who have no secrets from each other never want [or lack] subjects of conversations; they do not weigh their words because there is nothing to be kept back.
> —Francois Fenelon[11]

Mother Teresa had some amazing things to say about prayer that may help you and other God Chasers around the world:

> My secret is very simple: I pray. Through prayer I become one in love with Christ. I realize that praying to Him is loving Him.
>
> In reality, there is only one true prayer, only one substantial prayer: Christ Himself. There is only one voice that rises above the face of the earth: the voice of Christ. *Perfect prayer does not consist in many words, but in the fervor of the desire that raises the heart to Jesus.*
>
> Love to pray. Feel the need to pray often during the day. Prayer enlarges the heart until it is capable of containing God's gift of Himself. Ask and seek and your heart will grow big enough to receive Him and keep Him as your own.[12]

———

PRAYER OF HUNGER

I'm hungry for You
I'm hungry for You
I need Your touch
I see Your face
I need Your presence

When I wake up in the morning
I speak Your name
Even when I lay my head to rest
I need You there.
Here in Your presence
Is where I want to be
Lord, draw me closer
So much closer to Thee.

I'm desperate for You . . .
I'm longing for You . . .[13]

CHAPTER 5

PRAYERS *for* WISDOM AND GUIDANCE

WE DO NOT KNOW WHAT TO DO, BUT OUR

EYES ARE UPON YOU.

2 CHRONICLES 20:12B NIV

———

Things couldn't have looked bleaker for Judah and Jerusalem. King Jehoshaphat felt outnumbered, outmatched, and out of time. He had just left the best worship service in memory, and it was held in Jerusalem's new temple with the new ministerial staff and worship team in their places.

Then came the startling news: their sworn enemies from Moab and Ammon were on the warpath again, and they had even brought along some extra friends from Mount Seir to help in the fight. That meant that at least two armies were on their way and hungry for conquest. It was almost as if they had heard about the great church service and revival breaking out. They seemed determined to put a stop to it all.

The Bible says the concerned king "set himself to seek the Lord, and proclaimed a fast throughout all Judah. So Judah gathered together to ask help from the Lord; and from all the cities of Judah they came to seek the Lord."[1] (What would happen if more churches would do the same in times of crisis?)

After the king recalled God's promise to hear their cries in times of desperate need, he prayed passionate words that described the bankruptcy of his resources and the wealth of the nation's faith in God:

"*We have no power* against this great multitude that is coming against us; *nor do we know what to do, but our eyes are upon You.*" Now all Judah, with their little ones, their wives, and their children, stood before the Lord.[2]

It's okay to pray that prayer if you follow it up with, "*. . . but my eyes are on You!*"

> Have you ever felt like praying, "I don't know what to do"?

THE BATTLE IS NOT YOURS, BUT GOD'S

King Jehoshaphat's remarkable prayer was answered with a still more remarkable answer. It was the kind of divine answer everyone hopes to receive when they find themselves hemmed in by enemies or confronted with impossible circumstances.

This is what the Lord says to you: *"Do not be afraid or discouraged* because of this vast army. *For the battle is not yours, but God's. . . . You will not have to fight this battle. Take up your positions; stand firm and see the deliverance the Lord will give you.*"[3]

"So God answered an old king's prayer about some armies threatening his country . . . but what about the 'small' things in *my* life?" Many of us think God is far too busy to bother with our minor crises and questions, but it isn't true. I read somewhere, "[Cast] *all* your care on Him, for He cares for you."[4]

Our heavenly Father uses *every opportunity* to draw us to himself, even if it is a minor inconvenience or personal weakness that leads us to ask for His help. You and I both know that we "chase" Him only because He allows himself (or *actively arranges*) to be "caught."

God so appreciated the thoughtful prayer of one Old Testament bondservant seeking divine guidance that He eternally preserved the memory of his prayer in His Word. Why? Because this servant was wise enough to seek God for wisdom and guidance before attempting to obey Abraham's personal request.

HE SENSED ETERNAL DESTINY AND PRAYED FOR GUIDANCE

The man must have sensed that eternal destiny hinged on his ability to "access grace" and receive clear direction from his master's God:

Then he said, "O Lord God of my master Abraham, *please give me success this day,* and show kindness to my master Abraham.

Behold, here I stand by the well of water, and the daughters of the men of the city are coming out to draw water. Now let it be that the young woman to whom I say, 'Please let down your pitcher that I may drink,' and she says, 'Drink, and I will also give your camels a drink'; *let her be the one You have appointed for Your servant Isaac. . . .* And it happened, before he had finished speaking, that behold, Rebekah . . . came out with her pitcher on her shoulder. Now the young woman was very beautiful to behold.[5]

The story goes on to become one of the most beautiful and romantic love stories in human history. Rebekah's marriage to Isaac, Abraham's son, helped give birth to a nation and set up the continuation of the messianic line descended through their son Jacob/Israel.

As the father of three beautiful daughters, I would dearly love to find a man I could send out to find godly husbands for them with the same level of success. However, I have the feeling my daughters will prefer to use their *own* discernment and pray their own prayers in the matter— and seek my blessings in the process. (But I'm *still praying* for three God-ordained sons-in-law.)

PRAY FOR HELP BALANCING DAILY PRESSURE AND YOUR ETERNAL DESTINY

At times we must ask God for wisdom simply to manage the weight of the past and properly balance the pressures of today against our destiny for tomorrow. Frank MacNutt's brief prayer seems to say it all: "O Lord, forgive me for what I have been, sanctify what I am, and order what I shall be."[6]

At other times the Enemy of your soul sends such a bold challenge against all that you believe and so insults the God you serve that you just have to "show Daddy" what he said. This is the time to "spread out a letter before the Lord" as King Hezekiah did and give your problems to God.

> And Hezekiah received the letter from the hand of the messengers, and read it; and Hezekiah went up to the house of the Lord, and *spread it before the Lord*. Then Hezekiah prayed before the Lord. . . .
>
> "Hear the words of Sennacherib, which he has sent to reproach the living God . . . save us from his hand, that all the kingdoms of the earth may know that You are the Lord God, You alone."[7]

I HAVE HEARD

God told the king through the prophet Isaiah that because he prayed to God for help, "I have heard."[8] The Lord said the Assyrian army would *not* enter Jerusalem or shoot a single arrow. Not one shield or siege device would be seen from Jerusalem's walls, and the Assyrian king would go back home on the same path he had come *because God himself would defend the city*.

The Bible says an angel of the Lord killed one hundred eighty-five thousand Assyrian soldiers in their beds that night, and the few survivors awoke the following morning to find their camps filled with corpses.

The Assyrian king made a hasty retreat back home and went to worship his false god in Nineveh and was murdered by two of his own sons![9]

Many times we run into trouble because we *assume* God will handle things the same way He did at other times in our lives. David experienced unequaled success as a military commander, king, and spiritual leader, in part because he rarely assumed things with God. He seemed to be constantly seeking God for wisdom about tactics for battles.

Immediately after Israel finally crowned David king (he was already the king of Judah by then), the Philistines decided it was the ideal time to attack. David "inquired of the Lord" and was told to "go up" and fight, and he did. They defeated the Philistines *and* took away the idols they'd left behind.[10]

The Philistines didn't learn enough from the first battle, so they went up once again and redeployed their troops. Most people would have followed the same game plan that worked the time before, but David decided to ask God for a plan—even though he was facing the *same* enemy at the *same* place he had met them earlier. This time God told David *not* to go directly into battle. He was to listen for the "sound of marching" in the trees and then circle around *behind* the enemy.[11]

IT PAYS TO PRAY EVERY TIME

I believe the sound of marching distracted the Philistines and covered the sounds of David's forces moving to the rear. God also said that *He* would strike the Philistine camp. David obeyed, and Israel won a great victory that day. It pays to pray *every time* rather than only occasionally.

Richard Foster wrote this nugget of wisdom to help guide our search for divine wisdom and guidance in prayer:

Healthy prayer necessitates frequent experiences of the common, earthy, run-of-the-mill variety. Like walks, and talks, and good wholesome laughter. Like work in the yard, and chitchatting with the neighbors, and washing windows. Like loving our spouse, and playing with our kids, and working with our colleagues. *To be spiritually fit to scale the Himalayas of the spirit, we need regular exercise in the hills and valleys of ordinary life.*[12]

Learn to lean on Him at *all* times and He will help you in crisis times.

> It pays to pray *every time* rather than only occasionally.

I've noticed that the people with the most valuable insights into prayers for wisdom are those who depended on divine wisdom to survive. The Moravians of the sixteenth and seventeenth centuries managed to invade a world that was mostly hostile to their faith with what I will call the "normal Christian life." Their infectious joy in Christ had such influence that entire nations and continents experienced historic revivals because of the people they affected.[13]

The Moravian community was composed of people from many different church and theological backgrounds, but God transformed them through a supernatural visitation one day, and their faith was marked by such joy and continuing prayer that they became known as "The Happy People" in an age marked by the sour faces of Pietism. They boldly took their extraordinary faith and joy into the highways and byways of ordinary life.

Count Nicholas L. von Zinzendorf, the nobleman who gave shelter and divinely inspired leadership to the Moravian community, sought the Lord's guidance through his many challenges with these words of prayer:

PRAYER FOR
WISDOM AND GUIDANCE

Jesus, lead the way
Through our life's long day;
When at times the way is cheerless,
Help us follow, calm and fearless;
Guide us by Your hand
To the promised land.

Jesus be our light,
In the midst of night;
Let not faithless fear o'ertake us;

Let not faith and hope forsake us;
May we feel You near
As we worship here.

When in deepest grief,
Strengthen our belief;
When temptations come alluring,
Make us patient and enduring;
Lord, we seek Your grace
In this holy place.

Jesus, still lead on,
Till our rest be won;
If You lead us through rough places,
Grant us Your redeeming graces.
When our course is o'er,
Open heaven's door.[14]

CHAPTER 6

PRAYERS

of INTERCESSION

"FATHER, FORGIVE THEM, FOR THEY DO NOT

KNOW WHAT THEY DO."

Luke 23:34

≡≡≡

Jesus prayed this intercessory prayer for the very men who launched a cycle of violence and senseless torture so brutal that He would not survive it. These unforgettable words didn't come in an air-conditioned auditorium, in an outside amphitheater, or even in a rugged handmade worship structure perched on some Central American hillside among coffee plants.

These unmatched words of intercessory prayer came between desperate groans, through the crushed and bloody lips of a man only moments from death. Jesus uttered the greatest of all intercessory prayers from the cross while praying to the heavenly Father for the souls of those who had accused, battered, and abused Him without cause.

It seems obvious to me that Jesus was praying for more than the actual executioners from the Roman occupation force. He prayed for the Jewish leaders who provoked His crucifixion along with the Jewish hecklers, the Gentile onlookers, and every human being ever born since the Garden of Eden.

The Lord entered the depths of intercession and took upon himself all the sin and pains and burdens of the human race to carry them to the cross for eternal removal. It was the highest and greatest act of intercession the world will ever know. Jesus set the mark for all of us who follow in His footsteps as disciples and intercessors in this world.[1]

THE HOLY NUDGE

Have you felt the holy nudge lately to pray for those who misuse and abuse you or who reject everything you believe in? Did you yield to the press of the Spirit or did you shrug it off and move on with your schedule or personal agenda?

By any honest measure, I am the product of generations of intercessory prayer offered on my behalf by my father and mother, by my grandparents, and by my great-grandparents. My mother is a prayer *warrior*, and frankly, I wouldn't want to face her on the wrong side of a spiritual conflict. My mother has prayed fiercely and faithfully over my wife and me and over our children for decades.

Where would this world be without intercessor mothers who refuse to give up, shut up, or sit down until a matter of prayer is settled? (My fervent prayer is that the mothers from the newest generation receive the fierce spirit of intercessory prayer carried in hearts of more mature mothers in the church!)

Intercessory prayer possesses a purity that exceeds virtually every other form of prayer (the possible exceptions are those prayers of praise and worship offered directly to God). The virtue of intercessory prayer—its quality of exhibiting selfless care for others more than for our own needs and wants—elevates it above the rest.

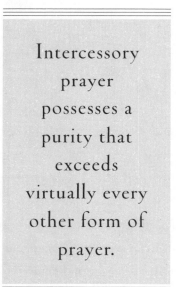

Intercessory prayer possesses a purity that exceeds virtually every other form of prayer.

My heart breaks over and over again when I realize that Jesus, the Lover of my soul, took up the eternal task of interceding to the Father on our behalf when He finally returned to His Father's side in heaven. I realize that He has many names and many duties and areas of authority in heaven, but He chose to place His high priestly role as intercessor at the forefront: "Who is he who condemns? It is Christ who died, and furthermore is also risen, who is even at the right hand of God, who also makes intercession for us."[2]

Some people carry the silent conviction that intercessory prayer is all but useless. It appears—I say *appears*—to be the opposite of action and forceful intervention in human events. If that is true, then why did the most forceful Being and Divine Intervener ever to walk the earth choose the job title of Intercessor when offered the opportunity to take His seat at the Father's right hand once again? Personally, I have a difficult time picturing Jesus Christ doing something "useless."

GREAT INTERCESSORS OF THE BIBLE

Many of the great leaders in the Bible were intercessors, because God made intercessory prayer a *mandatory* part of their ministry.

1. *Abraham prayed for a foreign king who took away Sarah, his wife.*

So Abraham prayed to God; and God healed [King] Abimelech, his wife, and his female servants. Then they bore children; for the Lord had closed up all the wombs of the house of [King] Abimelech because [he had taken] Sarah, Abraham's wife.[3]

2. *Moses often interceded for Israel—once for forty days and forty nights.*

Therefore the people came to Moses, and said, "We have sinned, for we have spoken against the Lord and against you; pray to the Lord that He take away the serpents from us." *So Moses prayed for the people.*[4]

And I fell down before the Lord, as at the first, *forty days and forty nights; I neither ate bread nor drank water, because of all your sin* which you committed in doing wickedly in the sight of the Lord, to provoke Him to anger. For I was afraid of the anger and hot displeasure with which the Lord was angry with you, to destroy you. *But the Lord listened to me* at that time also. And the Lord was very angry with Aaron and would have destroyed him; *so I prayed for Aaron also* at the same time.[5]

3. *Elisha the prophet interceded for the dead son of the Shunammite woman.*

When Elisha came into the house, there was the child, lying dead on his bed. *He went in therefore, shut the door behind the two of them, and prayed to the Lord.* And he went up and lay on the child, and put his mouth on his mouth, his eyes on his eyes, and his hands on his hands; and he stretched himself out on the child, and the flesh of the child became warm. He returned and walked back and forth in the house, and again went up and stretched himself out on him; then the child sneezed seven times, and the child opened his eyes. And he called Gehazi and said, "Call this Shunammite woman." So he called her. And when she came in to him, he said, "Pick up your son."[6]

4. *Job interceded for his friends—even though they were counselors in need of counseling.*

And the Lord restored Job's losses *when he prayed for his friends.* Indeed the Lord gave Job twice as much as he had before.[7]

5. *Daniel interceded for Israel for twenty-one days.*

Then I set my face toward the Lord God to make request by prayer and supplications, with fasting, sackcloth, and ashes. . . . "O Lord, according to all Your righteousness, I pray, let Your anger and Your fury be turned away from Your city Jerusalem, Your holy mountain; because for our sins, and for the iniquities of our fathers, Jerusalem and Your people are a reproach to all those around us. Now therefore, our God, hear the prayer of Your servant, and his supplications, and for the Lord's sake cause Your face to shine on Your sanctuary, which is desolate. . . . *O Lord, hear! O Lord, forgive! O Lord, listen and act!* Do not delay for Your own sake, my God, for Your city and Your people are called by Your name."[8]

6. *Paul demonstrated a deep gift of intercession in virtually every letter he wrote to the churches.* One of his most powerful prayers is honored as "apostolic intercessory prayer" at its best:

> For this reason I bow my knees to the Father of our Lord Jesus Christ, from whom the whole family in heaven and earth is named, that He would grant you, according to the riches of His glory, to be strengthened with might through His Spirit in the inner man, that Christ may dwell in your hearts through faith; that you, being rooted and grounded in love, may be able to comprehend with all the saints what is the width and length and depth and height; to know the love of Christ which passes knowledge; that you may be filled with all the fullness of God. Now to Him who is able to do exceedingly abundantly above all that we ask or think, according to the power that works in us, to Him be glory in the church by Christ Jesus to all generations, forever and ever. Amen.[9]

7. *We see how Jesus intercedes for us by the way He prayed for Peter and His followers in general.*

> And the Lord said, "Simon, Simon! Indeed, Satan has asked for you, that he may sift you as wheat. But I have prayed for you, that your faith should not fail; and when you have returned to Me, strengthen your brethren."[10]

> Now I am no longer in the world, but these are in the world, and

I come to You. Holy Father, keep through Your name those whom You have given Me, that they may be one as We are. . . .

I do not pray for these alone, but also for those who will believe in Me through their word; that they all may be one, as You, Father, are in Me, and I in You; that they also may be one in Us, that the world may believe that You sent Me."[11]

INTERCESSION IS A KEY TO REVIVAL

Many of the greatest church leaders since the first century seemed to have been skilled and persistent intercessors. God used John Wesley to help spark the First Great Awakening that transformed the spiritual face of America. This fiery evangelist clearly recognized the power of prayer—especially where revival was concerned. He declared: "Give me 100 preachers *who fear nothing but sin and desire nothing but God,* and I care not a straw whether they be clergy or laymen, such alone will shake the gates of hell and set up the kingdom of Heaven on earth. *God does nothing but in answer to prayer.*"[12]

In John Maxwell's book *Partners in Prayer,* an evangelical pastor eloquently describes the *meager harvest of a prayerless church:* "In Acts chapter two, they prayed for ten days. Peter preached for ten minutes and 3,000 were saved. Today, churches pray for ten minutes, preach for ten days, and three get saved."[13]

INTERCESSION IS A KEY TO SPIRITUAL GROWTH

What does intercession have to do with my pursuit of God's presence? The answer is simple: If you love Him, you will do everything you can to do His will and grant His every request. If you must become an intercessor to follow Him, then an intercessor is birthed. Sometimes intercession is seasonal. But that doesn't mean that we stop praying when the prayer is answered or the burden is lifted.

God commands us to "pray without ceasing."[14] I doubt if the command refers to praying unceasingly about our own laundry list of wants and needs. If the prayers of Jesus offer any guidelines, *intercessory prayer* is at the top of the list immediately below thanksgiving, praise, and worship.

Some may find it hard to believe, but the Holy Spirit takes great delight in "praying the Father's will" into existence on the earth *for us* and *through us*. The Bible describes the process this way:

> If you must become an intercessor to follow Him, then an intercessor is birthed.

Likewise the Spirit also helps in our weaknesses. For *we do not know what we should pray for as we ought, but the Spirit Himself makes intercession for us* with groanings which cannot be uttered. Now He who searches the hearts knows what the mind of the Spirit is, because

He makes intercession for the saints according to the will of God.[15]

Just how does the Divine Pursued One pray through the human pursuer? Watchman Nee described what happens when the Holy Spirit lays a "burden" on the heart of a God Chaser:

> When we are moved by the Holy Spirit our own spirit instantly senses a burden as though something were being laid on our heart. *After we pray it out we feel relieved as though having a heavy stone removed off us.* But in case we do not pour it out in prayer, we will get the feeling of something not yet done. If we do not pray it out we are not in harmony with God's heart. Were we to be faithful in prayer, that is to say, were we to pray as soon as the burden comes upon us, prayer would not become a weight, it would instead be light and pleasant.[16]

Thomas à Kempis, a German writer and Augustinian monk from the thirteenth century, penetrated the veil of religion to urge all who would listen: "Those who would be Christians must imitate Christ."[17] He wrote a powerful intercessory prayer that still serves as an excellent "borrowed thank-you card" to help us pray effectively for others.

Join me and pray this prayer from the heart before you move on to other things:

A PRAYER OF INTERCESSION

I offer up unto Thee my prayers and intercessions, for those especially who have in any matter hurt, grieved, or found fault with me or who have done me any damage or displeasure; for all those also whom, at any time, I have vexed, troubled, burdened, and scandalized, by words or deeds, knowingly or in ignorance: that Thou wouldst grant us all equally pardon for our sins and for our offenses against each other.

Take away from our hearts, O Lord, all suspiciousness, indignation, wrath, and contention, and whatsoever may hurt charity and lessen brotherly love.

Have mercy, O Lord, have mercy on those that crave Thy mercy, give grace unto them that stand in need thereof, and make us such that we may be worthy to enjoy Thy grace and go forward to life eternal. Amen.[18]

CHAPTER 7

PRAYERS
of TOTAL SURRENDER

———

LET IT BE TO ME ACCORDING TO YOUR WORD.

M ARY THE MOTHER OF OUR L ORD, L UKE 1:38 B

———

FATHER, IF IT IS YOUR WILL,

TAKE THIS CUP AWAY FROM ME;

NEVERTHELESS NOT MY WILL,

BUT YOURS, BE DONE.

J ESUS C HRIST IN THE G ARDEN, L UKE 22:42

———

God's invasion of man's misery and the fulfillment of His salvation plan began and found fulfillment in prayers of total surrender. He launched the divine dream the day a young woman named Mary surrendered her future, her reputation, and even her anticipated marriage to God's will. The dream came to pass when Jesus surrendered himself totally to His destiny of death on the cross because of His love for the Father and His kingdom.

He still works His will in the earth through surrendered hearts, wills, bodies, and lives. For this reason, the prayer of total surrender is the prayer of choice for God Chasers of every generation, location, and vocation. As God becomes our chief desire, a burning passion for Him makes every gift or offering that falls short of *everything* seem hollow and meaningless.

The pursuit of Deity is costly—you may be asked to spend everything to draw closer to Him who *is* everything. Jesus paid the full price for our forgiveness and adoption into God's family. Will you pay the full price for deeper intimacy with Deity? It comes at a dear price. The closer you come to the fire of God, the less of you remains in the heat of His holiness and glory. The more you love Him, the more you will sacrifice to do His will.

A QUESTION THAT RARELY LEAVES YOU UNTOUCHED

Corrie ten Boom, one of the great Christians of the twentieth century, was a Dutch survivor of Ravensbruck, a notorious Nazi concentration camp during World War II. She alone survived while the rest of her family died after they were caught sheltering Jews in their Amsterdam home.

Corrie penned a simple "prayer question" that she repeated and prayed before audiences around the world until her death in 1983. To pray it and ask it is to invite a costly self-examination in the light of Jesus' work on the cross. It is a question that rarely leaves you untouched: *"Lord Jesus, you suffered for me—what am I suffering for you?"*[1]

Jesus Christ epitomizes total surrender to the will of the Father. He is the reason we can never say we lack a model or guide for the path of total surrender. His personal call to discipleship rings with the stunning cost of total surrender in prayer, in word, and in deed. *The Amplified Bible* puts it this way:

> And He said to all, If any person wills to come after Me, let him deny himself [disown himself, forget, lose sight of himself and his own interests, refuse and give up himself] and take up his cross daily and follow Me [cleave steadfastly to Me, conform wholly to My example in living and, if need be, in dying also].
>
> For whoever would preserve his life *and* save it will lose *and* destroy it, but whoever loses his life for My sake, he will preserve *and* save it [from the penalty of eternal death].[2]

It seems to me that most if not all of the great sacrifices and "surrenders of the soul" in history were founded upon and motivated by love rather than fear. Is there any doubt that Jesus' surrender of His will in the garden was birthed in His *love* for the Father and for us?

LOVE: DEEPLY INTERTWINED IN PRAYERS OF TOTAL SURRENDER

Total surrender to God begins in total love. I have read, "Perfect love casts out all fear."[3] Love is deeply intertwined in any prayer of total surrender. Richard Foster wrote:

> Loving is the syntax of prayer. To be effective pray-ers, we need to be effective lovers. In "The Rime of the Ancient Mariner," Samuel Coleridge declares, "He prayeth well, who loveth well." Coleridge, of

course, got this idea from the Bible, for its pages breathe the language of divine love. *Real prayer comes not from gritting our teeth but from falling in love.*[4]

Isaiah the prophet began his ministry as a highly educated and respected member of the royal court. Evidently life wasn't all that difficult for him, until the day he experienced an encounter with the manifest presence of God in the temple. When he heard the voice of the Lord say, "Whom shall I send, and who will go for Us?" he was moved with supernatural faith to answer:

"Here am I! Send me."[5]

SHOT INTO THE WORLD AS A MISSILE FROM HEAVEN

Isaiah's life and ministry were "ruined" the day God's presence moved in. He began to speak with new authority as God shot him into his world as a heaven-sent missile to challenge the greatest earthly powers and spiritual strongholds of his day.

When Isaiah said "Send me" in the temple of God, he had no idea it would catapult him out of the temple. He would land among the people, walking naked through his land for three years at one point as a living prophetic sign of what was coming for the entire nation.[6]

A twenty-six-year-old Welshman named Evan Roberts had no idea what was going to happen the day he knelt in a pre-service prayer meeting with other Bible students and yielded to the passion of the Holy Spirit in prayer:

Roberts . . . knelt with his arms stretched out, perspiration soaking his shirt as he agonized over committing himself to God. Finally he prayed aloud, "Bend me! Bend me! Bend me!" . . .

The motto of the revival in Wales was born out of Roberts' experience that day: "Bend the church and save the world." Though still young, this new evangelist was about to become God's agent to carry the spirit of revival throughout his homeland.[7]

SEND ME OR BEND ME—IT'S JUST THE SAME

Three months of intimate encounters with the presence of God further transformed Roberts until he burned with a vision of seeing one hundred thousand souls come to Christ. The vision came to pass, and the Welsh revival ultimately affected virtually every continent of the world. Whether you cry out, "I surrender!" or "Send me!" or "Bend me!" the results seem to be the same—God gets the glory.

> Paul "ruined everything" for casual Christianity when he demanded absolute surrender to God's purposes.

The apostle Paul burned with such passion for God that he often seemed to be the proverbial "square peg in a round hole" among elite religious circles. Nothing has changed. His bold challenges still grate on religiously correct nerves. He "ruined everything" for casual Christianity and lukewarm "easy-believism" when he demanded absolute surrender to God's purposes:

> For *you were bought at a price*; therefore glorify God in your body and in your spirit, which are God's.[8]
>
> I beseech you therefore, brethren, by the mercies of God, that you *present your bodies a living sacrifice*, holy, acceptable to God, which is your reasonable service.[9]

During the years when I served as the pastor of a particular congregation, I preached a sermon on the Lord's Prayer and said, "We have no right to pray 'Thy kingdom come' until we've prayed 'My kingdom go.' "

YOU TALK AS IF I SHOULD BE JUST LIKE JESUS!

One of the men in the congregation came up to me afterward and said with some frustration, "Pastor, you talk as if you want me to be just like Jesus!" I told him, "We tend to be intimidated by Jesus' perfection; nevertheless, God *does* expect us to be like Jesus."

Some people struggle with the idea of "totally surrendering" to anything (except possibly their own desires, appetites, and individual will). I find it ironic that even Ralph Waldo Emerson, a secular American transcendentalist philosopher, realized that everyone "surrenders" to something or someone—even if it is selfishness. He wrote:

"On Our Faces"

The gods we worship write their names on our faces, be sure of that. And *a man will worship something—have no doubt about that, either.* He may think that his tribute is paid in secret in the dark recesses of his heart—but it will [come] out. *That which dominates will determine his life and character.* Therefore, it behooves us to be careful what we worship, for *what we are worshipping we are becoming.*[10]

The wise man surrenders to God, who in turn gives us back our lives and His love and blessings as well. The first surrender He requires of you may well be to submit to the divine urge to pray.

Dale Salwak, the editor of one of the many books on prayer that I read while conducting research for this book, wrote in the preface of *The Power of Prayer*:

> What, then, is prayer? It is a way to make contact with God, to feel His presence more surely. "I can take my telescope and look millions and millions of miles into space," said Sir Isaac Newton, "*but I can lay it aside and go into my room, shut the door, get down on my knees in earnest prayer, and see more of heaven and get closer to God* than I can assisted by all the telescopes and material agencies on earth."
>
> And what a privilege it is to enter into the very presence of that love! "*We do so,*" says A. W. Tozer, "*because, and only because, He has first put an urge within us that spurs us to the pursuit.*"[11]

WHERE DOES THE PRAYER OF TOTAL SURRENDER COME IN?

Sometimes God's answer to our prayers for wisdom and guidance presents us with another challenge even greater than before. Once you know

God's specific will in a particular circumstance, you face the greater challenge of *doing it.* This is where the prayer of total surrender comes in.

Dwight L. Moody was a former traveling salesman who devoted his life to preaching the gospel. It is said that he covered one million miles and spoke to one hundred million people in his ministry (quite an accomplishment in the late 1800s before the days of air travel or speedy overland travel). He prayed a simple prayer of surrender that still carries life-changing power today.

Pray D. L. Moody's prayer of surrender with me as a fellow God Chaser in hot pursuit of the presence of God and the things that give Him pleasure:

———

THE PRAYER OF TOTAL SURRENDER

"Use Me"

Use me then, my Saviour, for whatever purpose, and in whatever way you may require. Here is my poor heart, an empty vessel; fill it with your grace. Here is my sinful and troubled soul; quicken it and refresh it with your love. Take my heart for your abode; my mouth to spread abroad the glory of your name; my love and all my powers, for the advancement of your believing people; and never suffer the steadfastness and confidence of my faith to abate; so that at all times I may be enabled from the heart to say, "Jesus needs me, and I am his."[12]

CHAPTER 8

PRAYERS

of INSPIRED FAITH
AND
DIVINE DECLARATION

═══

AGAIN HE SAID TO ME, "PROPHESY TO THESE

BONES, AND SAY TO THEM, 'O DRY BONES,

HEAR THE WORD OF THE LORD! THUS SAYS

THE LORD GOD TO THESE BONES: "SURELY I

WILL CAUSE BREATH TO ENTER INTO YOU,

AND YOU SHALL LIVE...."'"

SO I PROPHESIED AS I WAS COMMANDED;

AND AS I PROPHESIED, THERE WAS A NOISE,

AND SUDDENLY A RATTLING; AND THE

BONES CAME TOGETHER, BONE TO BONE.

EZEKIEL 37:4–5, 7

═══

The day the prophet Ezekiel uttered these words of divine declaration, I doubt that he felt as if he was "God's man of faith and power for the hour." The hand of the Lord had deposited him in the middle of a dry and relatively lifeless plain, far from human habitation.

I imagine his ears were filled with the sounds of moaning winds, and he felt the heat of the sun baking the top of his head and the subtle gritty taste of airborne sand in his mouth.

To put things in modern terms, he wasn't in "Kansas" anymore, and he wasn't in some glorious evangelistic crusade either. The only thing separating this experience from a nightmare experience was the presence of God. His presence, mingled with man's words prayed in faith, can turn a nightmare into a living dream.

God gave Ezekiel *divine words* and commanded him to prophesy or declare them to the graves in that desolate valley. Later God told the prophet to speak to the winds as well.

OBEY AND DECLARE GOD'S WORDS TO ACTIVATE AND RELEASE GOD'S WILL

The miracles didn't come to pass because of *Ezekiel's faith*, they came to pass because he obeyed and *declared God's words*. This, in turn, activated and released the power and purposes of God in the earth.

It seems to me that the church is standing in a dry valley at this hour, and God is giving us divine words to proclaim in divine declaration. It is time for a resurrection in the world, but it will take a new and rare level of prayer to see it come to pass.

This level of prayer is only granted to those who are intimately acquainted with the heart and will of God, for it requires them to *speak the words of God* with divinely delegated authority.

Ben Patterson defined the dilemma of the modern church with pain-ful accuracy:

> Already, at age nineteen, in the early '60s, I could identify with the statement of a somewhat disillusioned pastor: "*Wherever Paul went there were riots. Where I go, they serve tea.*" Was it possible that God could use me that way, if I prayed?[1]

It appears we barely carry enough of His presence in our lives and church meetings to disturb a tea party, let alone destroy the gates or por-tals of hell in our cities.

HAVE YOU EVER SPOKEN AS AN ORACLE OF GOD?

What might happen if we became creatures of unceasing prayer and passionate pursuit of God's presence? We may find ourselves speaking as oracles of God and mouthpieces of the divine will! Do you think I am making up this concept or creating some new and strange doctrine? I wouldn't even consider it. It was Peter the apostle who said:

> As each one has received a gift, minister it to one another, as good stewards of the manifold grace of God. *If anyone speaks, let him speak as the oracles of God. If anyone ministers, let him do it as with the ability which God supplies*, that in all things God may be glorified through Jesus Christ, to whom belong the glory and the dominion forever and ever. Amen.[2]

Peter and John stepped into this "prayer of divine declaration" the day they met the crippled man at the "Gate Beautiful" of Herod's temple in Jerusalem. In that moment they didn't pray for the man's healing, although that is perfectly biblical and acceptable. They didn't ask God for wisdom in the matter, because they already knew His mind in that moment of divine appointment. The Holy Spirit had transformed their hearts and possessed their lives.

> What might happen if we became creatures of unceasing prayer and passionate pursuit of God's presence?

Peter fixed his eyes on that professional beggar and simply reached out and said in divine declaration: " 'Silver and gold have I none; but such as I have give I thee: *In the name of Jesus Christ of Nazareth rise up and walk.*' And he took him by the right hand, and lifted him up: and immediately his feet and ankle bones received strength."[3]

PETER SIMPLY DECLARED THE DIVINE WILL OF GOD

Intimacy with God produces union with His will and purpose. Passionate pursuit produces divine pregnancy in our hearts and supernatural fruit in our lives. Doubt had no place in Peter and John that day. Peter simply declared the divine will of God, and it came to pass instantly.

Since the miracle occurred on the Sabbath, it infuriated the "order keepers" of the Sanhedrin. After the religious officials arrested, threatened, and ordered the two men not to speak the name of Jesus in public, the apostles returned to their brethren, and the whole assembly prayed this *foundation-shaking declarative prayer for boldness* in unity:

> "Now, Lord, look on their threats, and grant to Your servants that with all boldness they may speak Your word, by stretching out Your hand to heal, and that signs and wonders may be done through the name of Your holy Servant Jesus." *And when they had prayed, the place where they were assembled together was shaken; and they were all filled* with the Holy Spirit, and they spoke the word of God with boldness.[4]

Why don't we see this kind of boldness in our churches today? Why are so few meetings "shaken and filled"? Where are the God Chasers who walk so closely with God that they transcend the limitations of their humanity and become the instruments of the divine will on the earth?

THIS PRAYER TRANSCENDS REQUESTS AND PETITIONS

When we become so surrendered to God that we become less and He becomes more,[5] He often speaks through us as *oracles* of God in prophetic declaration. This type of prayer transcends requests and petitions in prayer—it qualifies as a divine answer to prayer spoken through human lips (so there is no room or place for presumption here).

When the Spirit of God hovered over the congregation in Houston, Texas, as I stood in the back of the auditorium in holy expectancy, the pastor stood up under the anointing of the Holy Spirit. He quoted the familiar passage in 2 Chronicles 7:14 as he had many times before, but this time he spoke it with authority as a prophetic declaration of God's "now" will for that time, that place, and those people: "If my people, who are called by my name, will humble themselves and pray and seek my face and turn from their wicked ways, then will I hear from heaven and will forgive their sin and will heal their land" (NIV).

After quoting the passage, the pastor added, "I believe it is time for us to seek God's face instead of His hand . . ." *and he didn't get to say* another word. The "heavens opened and the earth split!"

God's tangible glory suddenly seemed to descend over the pastor and the entire congregation. Hundreds of us who were there felt overwhelmed by God's glory, and it changed my life forever.

Something similar happened in a Baptist church in Springdale, Arkansas,

> "I believe it is time for us to seek God's face instead of His hand . . ."

in 1995. The pastor, Dr. Ronnie Floyd, had just completed a forty-day fast at God's command. He made what I would call a prophetic declaration to his church at the end of the fast. He said, "I wrote the entire membership, encouraging them to be in our church on Sunday, June 4, 1995, *because I believed that it would be one of the monumental days in our church's 125 years of existence.* I told them that I was going to speak on forty days that changed my life."[6]

Within moments of worship, I sensed the Holy Spirit usher Himself into that room like a tidal wave. The power was unbelievable! On that morning, I repented of my sins. I stood in complete transparency before my people. I appealed to them to get their lives right with God so that revival could come into our church.

On that morning, our service lasted two and one-half hours. No one moved or left early. Time meant nothing because the Spirit of God was present among us. People were on their faces before God even before the public invitation began. Worship was powerful before the message and after the invitation. Incredible brokenness came upon the congregation. On that day revival came to the First Baptist Church of Springdale, Arkansas. . . .

On that day, the church got a new pastor without changing pastors. On that day, I got a new church without changing churches. When God comes, things are never the same again.[7]

The prayer of divine declaration is often preceded by uninhibited praise and worship to God. A. W. Pink, a highly respected Bible teacher, made an astounding observation about worship and the most powerful prophetic declarations made on earth or in heaven:

How blessed is this, that before any announcement is made of the awful judgments described in the Apocalypse, before a trumpet of doom is sounded, before a vial of God's wrath is poured on the earth, the saints (by John's inspired benediction) are *first* heard lauding in song the Lamb:

Unto Him that loved us, and washed us from our sins in his own blood, And hath made us kings and priests [not unto ourselves, but] unto God and his Father [for his honor]; to him be glory and dominion for ever and ever. Amen![8]

Worship took precedence—even in the closing moments of time!

SEEK HIS FACE, PRAY AT HIS FEET, AND STAND TALL

Intimacy with God produces authority with men and the inhabitants of the fallen spirit world. The more you seek His face, worship His glory, and pray at His feet, the taller you will stand when the time comes to "stand up and be counted."

You must invest *time* with God to experience *intimacy* with Him. That brings us back to the timeless topic of prayer, and this arresting exhortation of E. M. Bounds:

Christ wrote nothing while living. Memoranda, notes, sermon writing, sermon making, were alien to him. Autobiography was not to his taste. The Revelation of John was his last utterance. In that book we have pictured the great importance, the priceless value, and the high position which prayer obtains in the movements, history, and unfolding progress of God's church in this world. We have this pictured in Revelation 8:3–5. . . .

Praying men are essential to Almighty God in all his plans and purposes. *God's secrets, councils, and cause have never been committed to prayerless men.* Neglect of prayer has always brought loss of faith, loss of love, and loss of prayer. Failure to pray has been the baneful, inevitable cause of backsliding and estrangement from God. Prayerless men have stood in the way of God fulfilling his Word and doing his will on earth. They tie the divine hands and interfere with God in his gracious designs. *As praying men are a help to God, so prayerless men are a hindrance to Him.*[9]

George Fox, a founder of the Quaker movement (Society of Friends) in the seventeenth century, constantly urged believers to enter into an intimate and vibrant personal relationship with God. His letters to Quakers facing possible persecution radiate the authority of relationship to Deity in prophetic declaration. This is the language of a God Chaser in hot pursuit of his Beloved:

Sing and rejoice you children of the Day and of the Light. For the Lord is at work in this thick night of darkness that may be felt. Truth does flourish as the rose, the lilies do grow among the thorns, the plants atop of the hills, and upon them the lambs do skip and play.

Never heed the tempests nor the storms, floods or rains, for the Seed, Christ, is over all and does reign.

And so, be of good faith and valiant for the Truth. *For the Truth can live in the jails. Fear not the loss of the fleece, for it will grow again.*

And follow the Lamb, if it be under the beast's horns or under the beast's heels, for the Lamb shall have the victory over them all.[10]

YOUR SWORD IS NOTHING TO ME!

Richard Foster said a drunken soldier once put a sword to the throat of George Fox and demanded that he stop preaching. "Fox looked straight at the man and declared, 'Hack away, your sword is nothing to me but a straw!' Dramatically, the power of God fell upon the soldier; he staggered backwards, fell to the ground, and was converted."[11]

Another God Chaser, named Paul, prayed what was perhaps one of the greatest apostolic declarations or inspired prayers over the church in his letter to believers in Ephesus. Absorb the anointed power of this declarative prayer into your heart as you receive it as a divine declaration over your own heart and life:

For this reason I bow my knees to the Father of our Lord Jesus Christ, from whom the whole family in heaven and earth is named, that He would grant you, according to the riches of His glory, to be strengthened with might through His Spirit in the inner man, that Christ may dwell in your hearts through faith; that you, being rooted and grounded in love, may be able to comprehend with all the saints what is the width and length and depth and height; to know the love of Christ which passes knowledge; that you may be filled with all the fullness of God. *Now to Him who is able to do exceedingly abundantly above all that we ask or think*, according to the power that works in us, *to Him be glory in the church by Christ Jesus to all generations,* forever and ever. Amen.[12]

THE SIXTY-FOUR-WORD PRAYER FOR FIRE

Elijah the prophet uttered one of the greatest prophetic declarations of the Old Testament when he delivered his "sixty-four-word prayer for fire" while surrounded by King Ahab's 450 priests of Baal and Jezebel's 400 priestesses of Asherah.[13] In my mind, that situation left the prophet very little room for "evang-elastic" error.

Elijah was past the point of asking God for wisdom or asking Him for shelter or a meal. He wasn't even interested in asking for healing. Prior prayer had set up the time for declarative prayer, for proclaiming the divine will in the face of demonic resistance!

"Lord God of Abraham, Isaac, and Israel, let it be known this day that You are God in Israel and I am Your servant, and that I have done all these things at Your word. *Hear me, O Lord, hear me, that this people may know that You are the Lord God, and that You have turned their hearts back to You again.*" Then the fire of the Lord fell and consumed the burnt sacrifice, and the wood and the stones and the dust, and it licked up the water that was in the trench. Now when all the people saw it, they fell on their faces; and they said, "The Lord, He is God! The Lord, He is God!"[14]

William Booth and the Salvation Army virtually immortalized Elijah's confrontational theme with the hymn "Send the Fire." These prayerful firebrands were God Chasers of the first order, who joyfully endured the taunts of the proud to extend the gospel of saving grace to the humble and broken throughout England and America.[15]

CAPTURE THE FIERY PASSION OF GOD'S HEART

God is calling the church to spring into flame and catch the world on fire in His name. The only way to capture the fiery passion of God's heart is to draw near His heart so He can impart His desires to us. Once we receive them, we can *speak them* into the earth with authority.

Before we pray, consider this personal encouragement and prayer penned by John Wesley to a friend and receive it as my encouragement spoken to you:

> Lord, fill my heart with passion from Your heart.

Have you received a gleam of light from above, a spark of faith? If you have, let it not go! Hold fast by his grace that earnest of your inheritance. Come just as you are, and come boldly to the throne of grace. You need not delay. Even now the bowels of Jesus yearn over you. What have you to do with tomorrow? I love you today. And how much more does he love you?[16]

Now pray this prayer together with me, and declare His divine will with all of the passion and longing you possess as a God Chaser and lover of God:

———

PRAYER OF FAITH AND DECLARATION

Lord, fill my heart with passion from Your heart. Fill my mind with the thoughts and principles of the mind of Christ. Fill my mouth with the words You wish me to speak, and strengthen my soul with the courage to declare them to the desert of death and prophesy them to the winds of adversity.

You have commanded me to speak, so I speak as an oracle of God with the ability You supply. You have anointed me to minister, so I serve with the humility of a servant and the love of my Savior.

I declare a season of resurrection, a season when the glory of God will fill the earth and Jesus Christ will be glorified through the Church. I release the healing power of the blood of the Lamb over my region to the glory of God.

I release the passion of God in my home, my church, and my city to open the heavens. I release the resurrection power of God to destroy the works of the Enemy and to raise up the lost souls of my city and region.

I declare with divinely delegated authority based on God's unchanging Word that Jesus Christ is Lord over my life and all that concerns me. To Him be the glory forever. Amen.

CHAPTER 9

PRAYERS
of STRUGGLE

"AND OFTEN HE HAS THROWN HIM BOTH INTO THE
FIRE AND INTO THE WATER TO DESTROY HIM. BUT
IF YOU CAN DO ANYTHING, HAVE COMPASSION ON
US AND HELP US." JESUS SAID TO HIM, "IF YOU CAN
BELIEVE, ALL THINGS ARE POSSIBLE TO HIM WHO
BELIEVES." IMMEDIATELY THE FATHER OF THE
CHILD CRIED OUT AND SAID WITH TEARS,
"LORD, I BELIEVE; HELP MY UNBELIEF!"

MARK 9:22–24

I n the ideal world of escapists and religious pretenders, every one of us approaches each day and each task with total confidence. In the Christian world, this translates to the alleged ability to always speak and pray perfectly, using faith-filled words expressing the perfect measure of faith that fills our hearts.

The reality of where we *really* are can be depressing at times.

A young mother struggles unsuccessfully to control her anger using the guidelines in the stack of parenting books at her bedside, but in the end she screams out in frustration and collapses in a heap of tears, while her little boy cries himself to sleep in another room.

Often the score seems lopsided. "Often . . . falls into the fire and often into the water."[1] It can appear to be "two-to-nothing" and destruction seems to be winning. Don't quit the game. Keep seeking; keep praying! Even when a win would seem "unbelievable"!

A preacher may battle guilt because he has to take some prescription painkillers to treat constant migraine headaches that threaten to incapacitate him. He is afraid he has become addicted to the pills.

In the Bible's typically blunt and honest account of the father with a demonized son, we see an agonized human being who knows he hasn't measured up. Yet according to Mark's Gospel, he cries out to Jesus, "Help my unbelief!"[2]

This is a prayer of struggle, the cry of a person trapped between the weakness of the flesh, a fallen mind, and the immeasurable power of a holy God.

With one breath he questions the power of Jesus to make a difference: "But *if* You can do anything."[3] With the next he cries out for help with his unbelief. Personally, I'm convinced we *all* pray prayers of struggle in crisis at one time or another (regardless of what we pretend we do when in front of others).

HE DIDN'T DOUBT GOD'S ABILITY, HE DOUBTED HIS WILLINGNESS

Another unnamed Bible character questioned Jesus in another way that is even more familiar to most Christians. He didn't doubt the power and ability of God to heal, cleanse, and deliver—he had another kind of doubt that we still battle today.

> When He had come down from the mountain, great multitudes followed Him. And behold, a leper came and worshiped Him, saying, "Lord, *if You are willing*, You can make me clean." Then Jesus put out His hand and touched him, saying, "*I am willing*; be cleansed." Immediately his leprosy was cleansed.[4]

This man may not have framed his words in the classic form of a prayer, but he was really crying out to the Lord from the pain of his struggle: "Am I *really worthy*? I know you can, but I am a leper—will you actually extend to me the same love and power you give to perfect people?"

The words were barely out of his mouth, "If You *will . . .*" when the Bible says Jesus defied the ritual laws of cleanliness and reached out to touch the leper in full view of the crowd that had followed Him down from a mountain. He was making the point that the law does not apply to Him who makes all things clean and whole with one touch.

The Lord knows how frail human faith can become in moments of crisis —He doesn't demand perfection; He requires dependence, trust, and

> The Lord doesn't demand perfection; He requires dependence, trust, and covenant connection.

covenant connection. In return, He offers us an unending supply of divine grace, mercy, and favor that we could never earn.

Another form of the prayer of struggle emerges when we "wrestle with God" over something He is determined to complete in our lives. Most Christians are familiar with Jacob's wrestling match with the Angel of the Lord that left him with a permanent limp, a new name, and a fresh lease on his destiny.

A MODERN JACOB WRESTLED WITH GOD AND LOST

Fewer people know that Duncan Campbell, the minister used by God in the Hebrides Revival, finally stepped into God's perfect will only after he *wrestled with God and lost*. This modern era Jacob was already England's most renowned and respected minister, but Campbell entered a divine wrestling match the day his teenage daughter innocently asked, "Dad, why doesn't God use you like He used to?"

He said, "I held my composure . . . until she left the room. When she did, I fell on my face and said, 'God, *she is right!*' " Campbell made some desperate vows that day, and God answered him three weeks later as he sat on a stage before thousands of people who had come to hear him speak: "Get up and go to the Hebrides Islands, to the Isle of Lewis."

"I said, 'God, I'm still supposed to speak in this conference,' and He said just as clearly as I've ever heard anything said, 'Duncan, on the floor of your study you promised Me that you would do whatever I asked you if I would give you back what you had. *If you will go, I will give it.*' "[5]

HE LEFT THE PLATFORM AND HEADED FOR THE HEBRIDES

Campbell explained as best he could and left the platform and made his way to the Hebrides Islands.

> Duncan Campbell wrestled with God over his destiny, and he rose from his tearstained carpet a changed man. Only a man with a limp could be trusted with what would later be called "the Hebrides revival."
>
> This "non-tongues-speaking, much-heart-breaking" revival swept an entire region and was nothing less than purely miraculous. It began in the brokenhearted prayers of persistent worshipers and was launched in Duncan Campbell's heart *the day he wrestled with God and lost.*[6]

Prayers of struggle may also enter our lives when death, disease, or chronic illness strike without warning. My editor and his wife entered what would become a long-term season of continuous prayers of struggle when their second son began to manifest some strange symptoms at the age of one year and lost his ability to speak.

Doctors confirmed he had a severe form of epilepsy (an allegedly incurable condition) and prescribed drug treatments to control the seizures. The parents prayed the prayer of faith, and churches around the country prayed prayers of agreement. Nevertheless, every night in their home brought a new round of battles as they walked endlessly around their son's room, cradling him and praying over him as seizures caused the boy to grow tense and jerk uncontrollably.

After two years passed with no improvement, God led the mother to information about a virtually unknown treatment for epilepsy using a special diet. Initiated under the supervision of the boy's neurologists, the diet immediately stopped the seizures, and two years later the boy resumed a normal diet with all neurological evidence of epilepsy totally healed and medically verified (the boy is still healed today at the age of ten).

With one genuine miracle thankfully received, the couple continues their prayers of struggle, asking God to also heal their son of autism (also considered an incurable condition) and restore his speech. *Still in the struggle" means "still eligible for victory."* If you quit, it is impossible to win!

PRAYERS OF STRUGGLE OFTEN CALL FOR "LONG-FORM FAITH"

Prayers of struggle often define the kind of prevailing, persistent prayer needed for situations and crises that refuse to yield to prayer lines, the prayers of church elders, and the occasional corporate prayers in the church. They call for a "long-form faith" that persistently chips at the rocks of adversity long after others would give up and go home.

Perhaps Job described this "long-form faith" best in his brief declaration in the midst of monumental struggle and pain:

> "Hold your peace with me, and let me speak, then let come on me what may! Why do I take my flesh in my teeth, and put my life in my hands? *Though He slay me, yet will I trust Him.*"[7]

My wife and I have prayed our own prayers of struggle over the years. One fairly recent struggle (among many) comes to mind. While en route to preach a weeklong conference in Illinois, my wife and I learned that one of our daughters was in great pain and headed for the emergency room back home.

We had to seek God quickly—we love all of our daughters far more than we love any ministry, but we sensed this sickness "was not unto death" and that it was meant to disrupt a divine appointment.

WE OFFERED MANY PRAYERS OF STRUGGLE, AND GOD MOVED

After we prayed together for our daughter, my wife took the next flight home, while I sadly boarded a plane for Illinois. We offered many prayers of struggle to God during that time of severe crisis, and He moved both at home and at the meetings in Illinois. The revelations revealed at the meeting formed the basis for my book *The God Catchers*,[8] and God's provision for our daughter brought her safely home and drew our family even closer.

> The God of Rest personally meets us and answers our prayers of struggle . . .

I am thankful that no matter how severe or long-term our prayers of struggle may be, the God of Rest personally meets us and answers our prayers of struggle with a faithfulness and tender love that passes all understanding.

Julian of Norwich wrote a prayer in the fourteenth century entitled "On Trusting God" that embodies this unconditional commitment in prayer:

> He said not: thou shalt not be tempted; thou shalt not be travailed; thou shalt not be afflicted. But He said: thou shalt not be overcome.
>
> God willeth that we take heed of these words and that we be ever strong in such trust, in weal and woe. For He loveth and enjoyeth us, and so willeth He that we love and enjoy Him and mightily trust in Him, and all shall be well.[9]

PRAY FOR OTHERS IN THE MIDST OF STRUGGLE

I pray that you are *not* in the throes of the prayer of struggle as you read these words, but if this is so, then I urge you to pray for others you know who *are also* in the middle of desperate struggles and challenges of faith.

Grace Noll Crowell offers a powerful and passionate prayer to help us frame our own prayers on behalf of others in the midst of struggle:

> *To those who have tried and seemingly have failed,*
> *Reach out, dear Lord, and comfort them today;*
> *For those whose hope has dimmed, whose faith has paled,*
> *Lift up some lighted heavenly torch, I pray.*

They are so frightened, Lord, reach out a hand.
They are so hurt and helpless; be their friend.
Baffled and blind, they do not understand—
They think this dark and tangled road the end.

Oh, touch to flame their hope that has burned low,
And strike with fire faith's ashes that are dead.
Let them walk proudly once again, and go
Seeking the sure and steadfast light ahead.

Help them to move among their fellow men
With courage to live, courage to try again.[10]

David the psalmist also wrote prayers of struggle in the midst of his suffering: "Whom have I in heaven but You? And there is none upon earth that I desire besides You. My flesh and my heart fail; But God is the strength of my heart and my portion forever."[11]

THOUSANDS OF DEVOUT CHRISTIANS STRUGGLE SILENTLY IN FAITH

In a culture accustomed to quick results, many Christians today have little patience or ability to endure "prolonged no's" or lengthy periods in the abyss of the unknown. Nevertheless, thousands of devout Christians struggle silently in faith with cancer raging in their bodies, with parents who lose even more of their beloved memories every day, or with the unknown future of children who have gone astray.

If you are in this in-between place, where faith is balanced against the reality of pain and uncertainty, you may appreciate this prayer of the nineteenth-century poet Christina Rossetti, who suffered from Graves' disease later in her life:

PRAYER OF STRUGGLE

O Lord, Jesus Christ,
who art as the shadow of a great rock
in a weary land,
who beholdest thy weak creatures
weary of labour, weary of pleasure,
weary of hope deferred, weary of self;
in thine abundant compassion,
and fellow feeling with us,
and unutterable tenderness,
bring us, we pray thee,
unto thy rest.[12]

CHAPTER 10

PRAYERS
of ADORATION

———

"TAKE ME AWAY WITH YOU—LET US HURRY!

LET THE KING BRING ME INTO HIS CHAMBERS.

WE REJOICE AND DELIGHT IN YOU;

WE WILL PRAISE YOUR LOVE MORE THAN WINE.

HOW RIGHT THEY ARE TO ADORE YOU!"

SONG OF SOLOMON 1:4 NIV

———

What prayers does God desire the most? Have you ever wondered if God has preferences in prayer? We know He delights in prayers of all kinds, but I strongly suspect that if there is a favorite "flavor" of prayer in God's infinite mind, then it may well be the most rare of prayers as well.

The words "adore" and "adoration" may be two of the most powerful words we have to describe the deep levels in intimacy we experience in God. To "adore" means "to worship or honor as a deity or as divine, to regard with loving admiration and devotion, to be extremely fond of, to revere."[1] Adoration is "the spontaneous yearning of the heart to worship, honor, magnify, and bless God."[2]

Does the Bible contain a clue as to Deity's favorite prayer? The Psalms contain some of the most passionate prayers in existence, and they all seem to be prayers of adoration or "unconditional love on display." When culture-bound "morality editors" weren't putting scissors to the Scriptures, the language of Solomon in the Song of Songs was often used to describe the passion of Christ for the church and the bride for the groom.

Even the apostle Paul echoed this view when he used the relationship between husbands and wives to describe Christ's passion for the church, but he managed to avoid the prudish priests' scissors most of the time.[3]

All of these witnesses seem to point to the fact that *prayers of adoration* may be the prayers God most desires. These witnesses also seem to confirm why these prayers are so rare—it *costs* us something to offer God adoration. We must die to self before we can give ourselves unconditionally to Him.

Somehow, some way, we must get beyond ourselves and our endless lists of needs, wants, and desires to simply love and adore Him for who He is. To seek His face more than His hands; to love the "Blesser" more than His blessings—this is the height of maturity and the lost art of adoration!

WHAT IS ADORATION?

While describing the conflict between Mary and Martha in the gospel accounts, I wrote in *Chasing God, Serving Man*, "A. W. Tozer said, 'Adoration is the lost art of worship in the church,' and God wants to see this aspect of worship restored to the Church. *What is adoration? Babies are our best tutors on the subject of adoration, but young children do a pretty good job too.*"[4]

Most of the things I've learned about adoration over the years have come through my three lovely daughters. God used the adoration my daughters showed toward me as their earthly father to teach me how to adore and worship Him as my heavenly Father.

> Three times I asked [my youngest daughter], "What do you want?" Each time she said, *"Nothing, Daddy. I just want you."* Finally I told her, "Come on, get in the van." We drove into town and I said, "What do you want, baby girl?" Once again she said, *"Nothing, Daddy. I just want you."*
>
> Then we pulled up in front of a much advertised toy store, and her eyes lit up. By that time my heart was so melted that what I wanted to do was just go in and say, "Okay, baby girl, just tell me *which half of the store* you want. You can have this half or that half, it doesn't matter." I said, "Pick out whatever you want!"
>
> Do you know what she got? A little bottle of soap bubbles with the round wand that you blow through to make floating bubbles. Suddenly it became really obvious that she really didn't want anything. *She had just wanted me!*[5]

Why was I so surprised that my little girl had such pure adoration and unconditional love for me? Little girls are known for their ability to melt their daddy's heart with love, and naturally I think my girls were the top three contenders. Yet even with my girls, those moments of pure adoration and *unconditional* love could never come often enough or last long enough.

ADORATION IS NEARLY EXTINCT IN MANY CHURCHES

Adoration is rare in our everyday world, and I am afraid it has become nearly extinct in many of the nation's churches and worship facilities. Most church congregations and individual believers make it clear that they love God, but most of us have a habit of approaching our Father with our hands out. It takes an extreme effort for us to worship God for fifteen minutes *without asking Him for something.*

Does God discourage the asking? No, He takes great delight in hearing and granting our prayers and in providing our daily needs. Yet He especially longs for those rare moments when prayers of adoration waft their way through the maze and tangle of our seemingly continuous "give me, bless me, help me" prayers.

God carefully and patiently listens to all of our prayers (unless they are asked amiss), but our prayers of adoration are the closest things we have to unadulterated love for Him.

> Prayers of adoration are the closest things we have to unadulterated love for Him.

It is a struggle through stubborn flesh and clouded soul to move past our needs, hurts, and prejudices and into the lower levels of thanksgiving, praise, and worship. It is hardest of all to reach the deepest level of love—the level of pure *adoration* for Him.

ADORATION MAY MAKE YOU AN OUTCAST IN A ROOM OF LESS PASSIONATE LOVERS

This level of love virtually always makes you an outcast in a room of less passionate lovers. There is nothing like passion showing up to make complacency stick out like a sore thumb. Yet your goal isn't to "show them up" or win some kind of merit badge. Your deepest desire is to commune with Him and communicate the deepest longings and loves of your heart directly to Him.

It drove John to lay his head on the Lord's chest at every occasion, even though he probably paid a dear price.[6] John and his brother James were so fiery and aggressive in nature when Jesus first called them to His side that he "gave [them] the name Boanerges, that is, 'Sons of Thunder.'" He also gave one other disciple called Cephas a nickname as well, and it seemed to stick: Peter.[7] For a man so bull-like, sudden, and ready to fight, it must have seemed almost humorous to see him curl up so close to the Master day after day. God's love can conquer anything and everything.

There are passages in the Song of Songs that are pure adoration encased in human language. The problem is that many of those passages have romantic overtones to them that push well beyond the comfort zones of most people in North America (men in particular). Perhaps we should get over it and realize that God put Solomon's Song of Songs in His Word on purpose, not by accident. Consider the first phrases in the Song: "Let him kiss me with the kisses of his mouth—for your love is more delightful than wine. Pleasing is the fragrance of your perfumes; your name is like perfume poured out. No wonder the maidens love you!"[8]

The closest thing to spiritual adoration the world sees is the romantic adoration of one lover for another. They can't seem to "drink in" enough of their beloved's face and form, even if the loving glances extend "beyond long" to the point of nausea for those looking on. Even a faint whiff of the perfume usually worn by their beloved one is enough to send them into a dream state, with all kinds of odd behavior bound to follow. (I'm having fun with it at the moment, but many people would dearly enjoy reliving the sheer thrill of their first love if only for a moment.) With God you *can* return to your first love![9]

THE PASSION OF ADORATION FOR GOD MAY CAUSE YOU TO DO THINGS . . .

This tells us several things about prayers of adoration. You should realize there is little "self-control" in this form of prayer. It may begin orderly enough, but the passion of adoration for God may well cause you to do and say things you normally wouldn't consider.

Richard Foster once attended a small writers' seminar but found himself pulled away by a hunger for something more than could be provided by good conversation, challenging topics, or peer discussion groups.

He traveled by car and foot to follow his heart to the top of a high granite thumb rising above a wilderness river. There he had an incredible adoration encounter in the presence of God that encompassed many different kinds of prayer:

> What happened next is difficult to put into words. With the roar of the river quickly swallowing up any cry my voice could make, I felt free to shout out my thanksgiving and praise to God. A spirit of adoration and celebration sprang up within me, and I started dancing to the tune of a heavenly drummer and singing words unknown to my conscious mind. I sang with my mind too—hymns and psalms springing up from distant memory as well as spiritual songs that cascaded down in impromptu splendor. Thanksgivings poured forth for all things great and small. Praises joined with the river in joyous exaltation. It felt like I was being invited to join, in my feeble way, into the ceaseless paean of praise that ascends before the throne of God.
>
> In the beginning the experience was wholly effervescent, but in time the exuberance began to give way to a whispered, "Holy! Holy! Holy!" Worship grew deeper, more fertile. I had begun by blessing the name of God and was finally reduced to breathing the name of God. Exaltation sank into adoration.[10]

AN ENCOUNTER TAKING YOU TO AND THROUGH THE DEPTHS OF ADORATION

This is a portrait of what happens when hunger for God's presence seizes your heart and you dare to follow it to its ultimate end. The Lord carefully engineers divine encounters with all God Chasers, and many of those encounters with Deity take them to and through the depths of adoration.

Prayers of adoration—the passionate variety rather than the bloodless intellectual breed—have not always been welcome in traditional church environments. Sometimes problems start because someone insists on reading a genuine prayer of adoration in the traditional "bloodless intellectual" style. Although I've never understood how someone could read passionate words aloud in such platonic and passionless ways, I love to imagine what would happen *if...*

> The Lord carefully engineers divine encounters with all God Chasers.

I can see the reading glasses perched motionless on the end of the nose with the sounds of the words barely escaping pursed lips and the unmoving face—but *what if God really showed up?* What if the reader found himself in God's presence and felt "undone" by His love? In my mind, I see the reading glasses askew as the reader dabs desperately at tear-rimmed eyes, and deep cries of joy, repentance, thanksgiving, and adoration erupt from his belly.

Can you imagine what some ushers would do to such a troublemaker in certain church settings? Perhaps, but I imagine the person wouldn't mind being removed as long as he could take that sense of God's presence with him!

The medieval mystics of the thirteenth and fourteenth centuries pursued a more intimate relationship with God than they could find in traditional church services. Some of them suffered severe persecution from the established church or became outcasts.

The messages about becoming passionate God Chasers and God Catchers aren't always welcomed with enthusiasm today either. Why? Perhaps it is because they often highlight certain aspects of modern church practices that seem to glorify humanity more than God.

I try to always remember: *Humanity can't do for me what Deity can.* Ask Bartimaeus. His friends couldn't do for him what thirty seconds in the presence of God could do.[11] Worry more about Him and less about them.

MANY TYPES OF PRAYER AND WORSHIP BLEND SEAMLESSLY INTO ONE CONTINUOUS ACT

I've devoted much of my time and energy to igniting a desire in the hearts of others to chase and pursue God's presence. The prayer of adoration nearly serves as a "photograph" of the entire process of pursuing God and of His allowing himself to be "caught" by us. It includes many types of prayer and worship blended seamlessly into one continuous act of loving pursuit after the Beloved.

As wonderful as it is, the prayer of adoration doesn't seem to come "naturally." Richard Foster said,

The Prayer of Adoration must be learned. It does not come automatically. Notice our own children! They do not need to be trained to ask for things . . . but to express thanks? That is a wholly different matter. What endless effort it takes to help our children cultivate a habit of gratitude.

The same thing is true for us. Thanksgiving, praise, adoration—these are seldom the first words in our minds . . . or on our lips.[12]

If we need a model for pure adoration today, it would be the example Jesus prophesied would never be forgotten. Perhaps the greatest act of adoration for Jesus Christ occurred in the crowded dining room of a distinguished religious leader in Jerusalem.

And behold, a woman in the city who was a sinner, when she knew that Jesus sat at the table in the Pharisee's house, brought an alabaster flask of fragrant oil, and stood at His feet behind Him weeping; and she began to wash His feet with her tears, and wiped them with the hair of her head; and she kissed His feet and anointed them with the fragrant oil.[13]

Other religious dignitaries attended the meal, but they didn't offer the adoration because they were too busy trying to catch Jesus in a heresy or win His approval. It seems all twelve of the disciples were there, but they were too busy contending for first position to offer Him adoration that day. They were too busy jostling for political position at the right hand or the left. Mary, alone, noticed that *no one was at His feet.*

SHE ADORED HIM WITHOUT
A WORD

Only this "sinful" woman offered her adoration to the Master that day, and the Bible record does not say she spoke a single word. She let her adoration do the talking as she broke her alabaster box of anointing oil and mingled her own tears with it to clean and anoint His feet.

Then this woman of public disapproval did the unspeakable—she wiped the oil and tears mixed with the refuse from the heavily traveled road *with her own hair.* It got worse. She sealed the act by *kissing His feet.* Yes, the Scriptures say she *kissed the feet of Jesus.* I can almost see the disciples and stuffy Pharisees squirming. (Don't start looking for your censor's scissors yet.)[14]

He desires our adoration and worship. Heaven's "hall of fame" is filled with the names of obscure people like the one leper who returned to thank God while nine never bothered. It will be filled with the names of people who so touched the heart and mind of God that he says, "I remember you. I know about you. Well done, My good and faithful servant."[15]

If we learn anything from the biblical record, it is that your prayers of adoration often prove embarrassing to others who feel they are too proud or respectable to offer the same gift to God publicly. As I wrote in *God's Eye View,* passion is often the uninvited guest.

[Mary] was the uninvited guest at a dinner that religious men were hosting for Jesus. I hate to admit it, but passion is often the uninvited guest at our religious worship meetings too. Passion stands reluctantly at the door saying, "I can't believe they had Him in this house and no one told me about it. I don't think I'm really welcome here."[16]

Before you pray, put your heart, mind, and soul through a "tune-up" by reading and applying the truths from this passage found in my book on Mary and Martha, *Chasing God, Serving Man*:

> God puts up with a lot just to get 30 seconds of pure adoration from His children.
>
> Why don't we dispense with the formalities and just gaze into His eyes? "How do you do that?" All I know is that the posture of your heart is more important than the posture of your body. Do what it takes to assume the Mary position of adoration. You may need to close your eyes to look into His eyes. You may be more comfortable kneeling, standing, or lying prostrate before Him. Do what you have to do to tell Him from your heart, "I love You."[17]

Pray from your heart and use what I've provided below only as a guide or "starter" for the journey. Once your eyes turn fully upon Him, He will lead you, draw you, or carry you the rest of the way into His inner chambers.

PRAYER OF ADORATION

There's no turning back now, Lord. It's too late for me. I've fallen for You, and I can't get enough of You any other way. I'm desperate for an encounter with You, for an all-out surrender at the face place that leaves me delightfully and permanently addicted to You. If my life becomes a depository for divine purpose, so be it. I'll carry Your dream to full term just for the privilege of seeing Your face.[18]

CHAPTER 11

PRAYERS
of EMPTYING

O n the day of your invitation to dine with the president of the United States at the White House, or with England's royal family at Buckingham Palace, would you first take a side trip to gorge yourself at the fast-food joint next door? Yet we come to God's banqueting table with fists full of junk food and hearts filled with less than the best. Then we expect Him to bless us with His best.

Does the Holy God really enjoy sharing living quarters with the spirit of pornography to the right, the spirit of unforgiveness in the basement, and the spirit of pride and lawlessness upstairs? It is time to empty our lives of everything God didn't put there.

How do we do it? The Holy Spirit makes special use of prayers of emptying to accomplish the task. This process is closely aligned to repentance, but it is different enough to merit its own space and emphasis. You see, many if not most of the things you "empty" from your life are *good things*, not sin.

If you want Him to plant more holy things in your life from His hand, then you must empty yourself of everything He *didn't* give you.

> It is said the average American speaks nine million words a year. Five million of those words are the words *I, me, my,* or *mine.* It is a staggering statistic. It tells you something about the spirit of the age in which we live. It is a selfish age. All truth is parallel. God's solution for selfishness is death to self. Why should we be surprised when God calls for selfless leaders in a selfish age?[1]

"And whoever desires to be first among you, let him be your slave; just as the Son of Man did not come to be served, but to serve, and to give His life a ransom for many" (Matthew 20:27–28).

"EMPTYING" IN EASTERN RELIGIONS HAS A DIFFERENT AIM

While a Christian empties things from his soul and mind to be filled with God's Word and Holy Spirit, the act of "emptying" understood and religiously practiced by followers of virtually every Eastern religion has a different aim. They believe the path to perfection is to empty the human soul of distractions, attractions, affections, passions, thoughts, and emotions of all kinds to reach "nirvana," a state of total emptiness and "union with the universe" in perfect balance. What they don't understand is that nature (and the spirit realm) abhors a vacuum.

The "universe" isn't an empty space. It is occupied by two rival (but not equal) kingdoms. The greater kingdom of God refuses to abuse the empty state of a human soul and would never force its King or His will upon the human heart.

The lesser kingdom of darkness has no problem using, abusing, and destroying everything it touches. Its dark and eternally angry rebel prince is like a voracious cancer. This archangel turned arch-adversary goes about "like a roaring lion, seeking whom he may devour."[2] Emptied human souls look like fresh meat hanging in Beelzebub's public market—it is sure to attract all the flies of hell.[3]

THEY DON'T SEEM TO HAVE A CLUE

Christians possess the one Truth and Savior worthy to put into the space of an emptied human soul, but many of them don't seem to have a clue about the need for prayers of emptying. Christians seem to think that once they get saved they can live like the devil on Saturday, pray prayers and sing like a saint on Sunday, and land in heaven on Monday.

I have this sneaking suspicion that the apostle Paul saw things differently. He said of himself, "I have been crucified with Christ; *it is no longer I who live, but Christ lives in me*."[4] This was one of the greatest "emptying" statements ever uttered. It should be a true God Chaser's continuing anthem every day and every moment of the chase. This seems to be the perfect mix and balance of "emptying" and "filling."

The world's concept of emptying can be incredibly dangerous, and no Christian should "empty" himself unless God is allowed to put something holy and wholesome in that space. Jesus warned:

> "When an unclean spirit goes out of a man, he goes through dry places, seeking rest; and finding none, he says, '*I will return* to my house from which I came.' And when he comes, *he finds it swept and put in order. Then he goes and takes with him seven other spirits more wicked than himself, and they enter* and dwell there; and *the last state* of that man is worse than the first."[5]

The real importance of *emptying* for Christians is found in *God's filling*. He wants to fill us with new revelations of himself, but first we must make room by removing all of the undesirable contents, belongings, and possessions (sometimes literal demonic possessions) of the "old man" who passed away before the Holy Spirit moved in.[6]

> He wants to fill us with new revelations of himself, but first we must make room.

DIVINE ENCOUNTERS NEARLY ALWAYS "COST" US SOMETHING

Without exception, human lives are always transformed by divine encounters. It is also true that those encounters nearly always "cost" us something.

Moses was "mighty in speech" until he turned 40 and tried to fulfill his destiny on his own. Then he had an intimate encounter with God that apparently left him a stutterer! Sometimes what we consider to be "religious eloquence" is really a "spiritual stutter," an impediment to true communication with and for the Almighty. . . .

We cannot pray, "Thy kingdom come . . ." unless first we are willing to pray, "My kingdom go. . . ." We have a tendency to hold onto "our kingdom" with a death grip, but we need to learn there is a power that comes through relinquishment.[7]

Sometimes the very strengths of your life before Christ become deficits after you surrender all to Him. On the other hand, your weaknesses become perfect strength in His hands.

And lest I should be exalted above measure by the abundance of the revelations, a thorn in the flesh was given to me, a messenger of Satan to buffet me, lest I be exalted above measure. Concerning this thing I pleaded with the Lord three times that it might depart from me. And He said to me, *"My grace is sufficient for you, for My strength is made perfect in weakness."*[8]

THE CREATION OF GODLY DEPENDENCE

One of the most important functions of prayers of emptying is the creation of *godly dependence* upon the faithfulness of God and deliverance from confidence in the flesh and in the human soul. The first attempt of Satan to subvert God's highest creation was based upon pride of place and independence from the Creator of all things. Things haven't changed much.

The stupidity of independence is as old as Adam and Eve. We must realize that we could not even breathe one breath, think one thought, or earn one dime without His blessing and empowerment. Anything less is presumption and rebellion. *The very taproot of rebellion is in the desire to be "great" on our own terms.* God's treatment and cure for the spirit of independence and rebellion in a believer is the discipline of relinquishment.[9]

PENETRATED BY THE SPIRIT OF GODWARD SURRENDER

A man of fervent faith and unyielding convictions, Ignatius of Loyola was imprisoned as a heretic in Spain. He was released and promptly made his way to France. He founded the "Company of Jesus" or the Jesuits to "provide a spiritual and intellectual foundation for Catholic renewal" in the face of Protestantism.

Regardless of modern opinions among Protestants about certain activities of the Jesuits since their order was founded more than five centuries ago, I'm convinced most of us recognize the depth of his words in this prayer of emptying penned long ago. They still penetrate body, soul, and spirit with the spirit of godward surrender:

Take, Lord, all my liberty,
my memory,

my understanding,
and my whole will.
You have given me all that I have,
all that I am,
and I surrender all to Your divine will,
that You dispose of me.
Give me only Your love and Your grace,
With this I am rich enough,
and I have no more to ask.
Amen.
—Ignatius of Loyola[10]

Long before God ever told Moses to throw his rod to the ground, to watch it turn into a serpent, or to pick it up again by the tail and see it return to the form of a rod, *God knew* what was waiting in Pharaoh's court.[11]

He knew every magic trick and act of sorcery possessed and practiced by the magicians and wise men in Pharaoh's court. The Almighty One knew Pharaoh's magicians would match the rod-turns-into-a-serpent trick, and He had already planned to upstage and embarrass them in front of Pharaoh.

MEET ONE OF THE BIBLE'S MOST RELUCTANT HEROES

Moses knew none of this, and at that early stage of his new ministry as a deliverer, he ranks as one of the Bible's most reluctant heroes. He must have been the most horrified of all the onlookers when Pharaoh's magicians threw down their rods and commanded them to become serpents. He probably held his breath until God caused His rod-become-a-serpent to literally consume *all* the serpent-rods of the magicians.[12]

Moses went forward in his *weakness*, not in his strength. He was learning how to empty himself so God could fill him up with His glory; and that was his qualification for unprecedented leadership under the old covenant.

Only your emptiness determines the amount of oil you will receive for the future. Don't be afraid to put your emptiness on display. Ask the little lady in 2 Kings 7 about the *value of her emptiness*.[13]

Arturo Toscanini was a famous Italian symphony conductor. His specialty was the works of Beethoven. One night in Philadelphia, Pennsylvania, Tuscani conducted the Philadelphia Symphony Orchestra in a program that included the Ninth Symphony, one of the most difficult pieces to direct. It was so majestic and so moving that when the piece was completed, the audience stood for round after round of applause. Tuscani took his bows again and again. He turned to the orchestra; they bowed. The audience continued to clap and cheer. The orchestra members themselves were smiling and clapping. Finally, Tuscani turned his back to the audience, and spoke only to the orchestra. He said, "Ladies, gentlemen—I am nothing. You are nothing. Beethoven is everything."

When you think of this story, remember the divine power of relinquishment. Regardless of how eloquent you are, or how gifted you are with a voice to sing like an angel, *throw yourself at the feet of Jesus and let Him take the serpent out of your gift.*[14]

FOCUS MORE ON HIS FILLING THAN ON YOUR EMPTYING

Prayers of emptying take many forms, but perhaps the highest form focuses more on His filling than on your emptying. A twelfth-century prayer attributed to St. Francis of Assisi seems to illustrate the point better than a book of less anointed words:

Lord, make me an instrument of Your peace.
Where there is hatred, let me sow love,
Where there is injury, pardon,
Where there is doubt, faith,
Where there is despair, hope,
Where there is darkness, light,
Where there is sadness, joy.

O Divine Master, grant that I may
Not so much seek to be consoled as to console,
Not so much to be understood as to understand,
Not so much to be loved as to love;

For it is in giving that we receive,
It is in pardoning that we are pardoned,
It is in dying that we awake to eternal life.
—St. Francis of Assisi[15]

HE LOVES US, BUT HE WANTS TO CRUCIFY US (AND RAISE US AGAIN)

Our Lord isn't interested in erasing or eradicating our individuality or our unique personality, but He does want to crucify it and raise it again in new birth without all the baggage of the old creature. It seems He said somewhere: "If anyone desires to come after Me, let him *deny himself*, and take up his cross daily, and follow Me. For whoever desires to save his life will lose it, but *whoever loses his life* for My sake will save it."[16] And: "Most assuredly, I say to you, unless one is *born again*, he cannot see the kingdom of God."[17]

GODLY EMPTYING BEGINS THE MOMENT YOU REPENT

Why would I quote "salvation" Scriptures in the middle of this chapter on prayers of emptying? It is because the godly emptying process begins right here—at the moment of repentance and spiritual regeneration. It doesn't start with a whimper or a counseling session; it starts with the same kind of supernatural explosion that rocketed Jesus out of the tomb on resurrection morning.[18]

> The godly emptying process begins at the moment of repentance and spiritual regeneration.

Erasmus was a leading scholar of the fourteenth and fifteenth centuries who seemed to understand the core truth of all emptying prayers—*self* is that which must be emptied from us the most. He wrote passionate writings protesting corruption in the Catholic Church of his era (he was himself

a Catholic believer), and his writings advocating religious peace and freedom were banned by two popes.

Many folks have wrestled with prayers of emptying over the centuries, and Erasmus is one of the few who really seemed to tap into God's
heart in this area. After you read and gauge its biblical nature for yourself,
I encourage you to pray this prayer of emptying with me, and then move
on to pray your own personalized prayers of emptying to the God of all
fullness:

PRAYER OF EMPTYING

Sever me from myself that I may be grateful to you;
may I perish to myself that I may be safe in you;
may I die to myself that I may live in you;
may I wither to myself that I may blossom in you;
may I be emptied of myself that I may abound in you;
may I be nothing to myself that I may be all to you.[19]

CHAPTER 12

PRAYERS

of COMMITMENT

"INTO YOUR HAND I COMMIT MY SPIRIT."

PSALM 31:5A

═══

M any generations after the great psalmist penned these prophetic words, one called "the Son of David" cried out with a passion that pierced the heart of the heavenly Father, uttering these same messi-anic words through wounded lips from a Roman cross stained with His own blood: *"Father, into Your hands I commit My spirit."*[1] No other prayer Jesus prayed would equal the power of this final prayer of commitment.

In the same way, I suspect no prayers of commitment uttered earlier in life will match our final prayer of commitment said moments before death as we exhale our last breath in the created world.

Remember that no true prayer of commitment can be made apart from God's grace. He is the only unchanging power in the universe, and it takes His power working in your life to help you keep a fixed promise in an ever-deteriorating world.

Prayers of commitment have the force of covenant in the kingdom of God. That means we should not make commitments to God lightly, because He takes them very seriously. He remembers every idle word we speak, even if we forget it moments after we leave the building or meeting atmosphere.[2]

The most important prayer of commitment you and I ever made was the "sinner's prayer" we prayed to receive Jesus Christ as Lord and Savior of our lives. It is the New Covenant reality of the covenant commitment foreshadowed in the biblical story of Ruth's unforgettable declaration to her mother-in-law, Naomi:

> "Entreat me not to leave you, or to turn back from following after you; for wherever you go, I will go; and wherever you lodge, I will lodge; Your people shall be my people, and your God, my God. Where you die, I will die, and there will I be buried. The Lord do so to me, and more also, if anything but death parts you and me."[3]

COMMITMENT CARRIES US BEYOND MERE INTENTION

Why is the issue of commitment important in a book on prayer? Commitment is the first *action* that carries us beyond *mere intention* to *do* the will of God. Most of the New Testament writing is devoted to moving us beyond mere intention to the actual *doing* of God's will. Unfortunately, we are far quicker to say a thing than we are to actually do it.

It reminds me of the particularly odd prayer exchange witnessed by my father in one of his countless meetings. A young man with a lot of zeal was praying loudly at the altar, *"Lord, fill me!"* At the same time an elderly woman next to him prayed just as loudly, *"Don't do it, Lord. He leaks!"*[4]

Evidently this young man was known for his habit of making passionate requests and commitments in the middle of exciting revival and prayer meetings and for losing or totally forgetting it all the following Monday.

We make prayers of commitment far more often than most of us realize. We make prayers of commitment for ourselves, for our marriages, for our families, for our churches, and even for our nation.

GOD CALLS FOR PRAYERS OF COMMITMENT

There is nothing wrong with making prayers of commitment. God in essence calls for a prayer of commitment every time the Holy Spirit convicts us of sin, exhorts us to action, or establishes direction or vision. Nearly all of these factors appeared the day Joshua challenged the Israelites on the "promised" side of the River Jordan:

> "Now therefore, fear the Lord, serve Him in sincerity and in truth, and put away the gods which your fathers served on the other side of the River and in Egypt. Serve the Lord! And if it seems evil to you to serve the Lord, *choose for yourselves this day whom you will serve*, whether the gods which your fathers served that were on the other side of the River, or the gods of the Amorites, in whose land you dwell. *But as for me and my house, we will serve the Lord."* [5]

The Christian life is a life of eternal commitment to the One who committed all for us. Our problem is that we make and hold our commitments too lightly.

John Wesley said, "What we need is a desire to know the whole will of God, with a fixed resolution to do it." Richard Foster used this quote to launch a remarkable chapter entitled "Covenant Prayer" in his book *Prayer: Finding the Heart's True Home.* Foster's concept of covenant prayer closely resembles what we call prayers of commitment:

> "My heart is fixed, O God, my heart is fixed."

The essence of Covenant Prayer is captured in the confession of the Psalmist: "My heart is fixed, O God, my heart is fixed" (Psalm 57:7 KJV). At the altar of Covenant Prayer we vow unswerving allegiance; we make high resolves; we promise holy obedience.

I can well imagine that you almost instinctively draw back from all this language of commitment. I draw back from it too. Why is this?

Well, first of all, many people today are simply not good at commitments of any kind. In one sense it is hardly our fault. It is in the air. It is the mood of the times. Commitment means responsibility, and responsibility sounds confining. . . .

Absolute freedom is absolute nonsense. We gain freedom in anything through commitment, discipline, and a fixed habit.[6]

The fires of persecution and adversity birth the greatest prayers of commitment in our lives. *We respond to God most purely and passionately when we need Him most desperately and urgently.*

Job uttered a prayer of commitment in the form of a spoken declaration when things looked their worst in his long trial of faith. It was in the midst of his pain—when all he could see was more sorrow on the horizon—that Job said: "Though He slay me, yet will I trust Him."[7]

In an age of disposable marriages and throwaway babies, commitment marches out of sync and out of style. Nevertheless, the eternal drumbeat of God's Word and will still sets the cadence.

WILL CHRISTIANS EVER LINE UP FOR SEMINARS ON COMMITMENT?

What would happen to modern Christianity (particularly in the West) if more of us exhibited this level of unconditional commitment to God? Will there ever be a day when Christians by the hundreds of thousands will mark their calendars, reserve their resources, and travel untold miles to attend conferences, seminars, or camp meetings based on the thoroughly biblical theme "Suffering and Adversity, and Praying Prayers of Commitment in the Midst of Them"?

We've already cited Hannah's passionate prayer for a child as an example of a prayer of desperation (chapter 2), and rightly so. Her plea for a child pierced the heavens after she had endured years of persecution from her husband's other wife, a woman who had already borne him many children.

It is likely that Hannah had prayed for children many times, even in the same location at the same time of year.[8] The *difference* between those prayers and the prayer God answered (and the reason I bring it up again) is that *this time Hannah prayed a prayer of commitment.*

Does this mean a commitment will induce or convince God to give you what you want? No, but God *does* pay attention to our commitments. It is possible that He guided Hannah to the point where she could add the component of commitment to her desperation. Perhaps God wanted Hannah to birth a prophet of God in prayer and commitment before He would allow her to give birth to Samuel in the physical sense.

Miles Coverdale also penned a powerful prayer of commitment in the fires of persecution. He was an Augustinian monk who dared to embrace the Protestant Reformation. He was exiled to Geneva from England during the reign of Mary I, or Mary Tudor (the Roman Catholic Queen of England, known as "Bloody Mary," who ruled from 1553 to 1558).

HE KNEW WHAT IT MEANT TO BE PERSECUTED

Coverdale translated the Scriptures and many of the writings of European reformers into the English of his day (against the will of Rome). He knew what it meant to be persecuted and to live under the constant threat and menace of imprisonment or physical danger. Yet he felt he had a mandate from God to help provide God's Word and the writings of key church leaders for the people.

This man exhibited the rare conviction that it was just as important to be Christlike in his daily attitudes as it was to accomplish "great things" in His name (too many of us feel that great sacrifices entitle us to harbor wrong attitudes, unforgiveness, and bitterness because we are "doing so much for Christ").

It was in the midst of genuine persecution, physical danger, and the constant threat of death that Coverdale penned this remarkable prayer of commitment:

"When Persecuted"

O God, give us patience when the wicked hurt us. O how impatient and angry we are when we think ourselves unjustly slandered, reviled and hurt! Christ suffers strokes upon his cheek, the innocent for the guilty; yet we may not abide one rough word for his sake. O Lord, grant us virtue and patience, power and strength, that we may take all adversity with good will, and with a gentle mind overcome it. And if necessity and your honour require us to speak, grant that we may do so with meekness and patience, that the truth and your glory may be defended, and our patience and steadfast continuance perceived.

—Miles Coverdale[9]

WE DISLIKE PERSONAL RESPONSIBILITY

Too many of us subdivide prayers of commitment into casual or virtually "thoughtless" prayers of commitment and "serious" ones. We mouth and forget hundreds of prayers in the first category (which still grieves the heart of God). Yet we carefully avoid the second kind, the serious prayers of commitment. Why? We fear the prospect of failure, and we dislike personal responsibility that cannot be discharged in one day, or a week at most.

Andrew Murray, the great apostle of prayer who wrote extensively and ministered throughout South Africa in the late 1800s and early twentieth century, wrote this powerful encouragement for commitment to God:

O Christian, only believe that there is a victorious life! Christ, the Victor, is your Lord, who will undertake for you in everything and will enable you to do all that the Father expects from you. Be of good courage. Will you not trust Him to do this great work for you, He who has given his life for you and has forgiven your sins? Only dare, in His power, to surrender yourself to the life of those who are kept from sin by the power of God. Along with the deepest conviction that there is no good in you, confess that you see in the Lord Jesus all the goodness you need for the life of a child of God, and begin literally to live "by the faith of the Son of God, who loved you, and gave himself for you."[10]

This is the secret to praying prayers of commitment. You and I are virtually unable to keep a single commitment to God *under our own strength*. Yet in *His* strength and faithfulness, in the words of Paul, we *"can do all things."*[11]

IT TAKES GOD'S HELP FROM BEGINNING TO END

The best way to appropriate or "make withdrawals" from God's heavenly accounts of faith, power, love, and grace is to hear His voice, respond to His commands, and dare to *believe* Him. Any divine request He makes of you is by definition *supernatural*. You cannot and will not fulfill a supernatural calling solely through natural strength, resources, or wisdom. It takes God's help from beginning to end.

The apostle Paul sums up the process in one sentence (italicized) while issuing a challenge to the first-century believers in Philippi in Asia Minor:

> Therefore, my beloved, as you have always obeyed, not as in my presence only, but now much more in my absence, work out your own salvation with fear and trembling; *for it is God who works in you both to will and to do for His good pleasure.* Do all things without complaining and disputing, that you may become blameless and harmless, children of God without fault in the midst of a crooked and perverse generation, among whom you shine as lights in the world, holding fast the word of life, so that I may rejoice in the day of Christ that I have not run in vain or labored in vain.[12]

Commitment is the foundation of everything that happens in the kingdom of God. It began with God's commitment of breath to Adam, and expanded to His commitment of His Garden into Adam's care. It reached a pinnacle on the cross at Calvary, where Jesus Christ became sin for us and committed His life into His Father's hands.

GRACE: GOD'S PROVISION FOR OUR TENDENCY TO FAIL, FALL, AND FALTER

God has made His commitment and kept His promises. When He asks you to make a commitment, He stands ready to help you overcome all fear and obstacles to make and keep your commitment to Him. He made provision for our tendency to fail, fall, and falter—it is called *grace*!

When God speaks to your heart about offering prayers of commitment, offer them in honesty. Mention the doubts you feel concerning your *own* ability to keep your promise, and express your faith in *His* ability to keep you, carry you, and lift you higher day after day. You grow stronger each time you offer a Spirit-breathed prayer of commitment and persevere until you see Him carry you through.

> Commitment is the foundation of everything that happens in the kingdom of God.

This is the process of growing faith and trust that God calls the abundant life. Dare to obey and trust Him; expect obedience to carry you far beyond your own ability and vision; and rejoice each time you discover His hand at work in your life. It is yet another proof that you are His child and that He is intimately involved in every detail of your progress toward and pursuit of His presence.

YOUR CHANGED LIFE IS A PROOF OF GOD'S EXISTENCE

This generation is desperately searching for proof of a loving God, and the most prominent and easily tested proof of God's existence in your neighborhood is *your changed life*.

People around you, who do not know God, *hope He exists*—but they won't take your word for it. They want to see proof in the form of a commitment no sane person would make if He did *not* exist.

You *know* He lives, and because He lives we know that death has lost its sting.[13] Your commitment to Him should be so strong that you no longer fear death as do those with no hope of the resurrection.

Your unconditional love for Him should transcend the trauma of accidents and the pain of disease and loss (just as His unconditional love transcends your tendency to sin and fail each day). We believe God heals, but will we love Him *anyway* if for unknown reasons He does not heal our cancer or deliver us from Alzheimer's disease?

Pray this prayer of commitment with me (if you're ready):

═══

PRAYER OF COMMITMENT

Lord, You made the highest commitment to me when
You laid down Your life for mine. Grant me the grace to

live a life wholly committed to You.

In my own strength, Lord, I am more likely to break my promises than to keep them, so I must lean on Your strength in the keeping of this commitment. In my own wisdom, Lord, I am more likely to go astray than to go aright at any given moment, so I seek Your wisdom more than my own.

In my own righteousness, I am more likely to sin than to win in the struggle for holy living before my friends and co-workers.

I made a commitment to You the day You received me as Your own. My heart longs for You, my mind thinks and meditates upon You; my body exists to serve You as an extension of Your hand to the lost, the lonely, the hurting, and the dying.

Into Your hands I commit my spirit, my soul, my body, and my destiny. My life is not my own for I have been bought with a price. I commit this day and every future day into Your hands as well. Glorify Yourself in me as I passionately pursue You with all of my heart, soul, body, and strength. I pray all of these things by faith in Jesus' name.

EPILOGUE:
YOUR PRAYERS OF PURSUIT

THEY SHOULD SEEK THE LORD, IN THE HOPE

THAT THEY MIGHT GROPE FOR HIM AND FIND

HIM, THOUGH HE IS NOT FAR FROM EACH ONE

OF US; FOR IN HIM WE LIVE AND MOVE

AND HAVE OUR BEING.

ACTS 17:27-28A

W e make prayer hard. It isn't; it becomes simple with practice in the same way driving a car becomes simple with practice. We considered praying hard work. It isn't. The hard part stems directly from the discipline or surrender required in the praying.

Except in the most extreme and extraordinary of circumstances, we communicate with others almost continually as we go about our daily activities. It follows that we should just as naturally communicate continuously with our spiritual Friend and unfailing Companion throughout each day.

Their types, forms, and methodology naturally flow with the needs, wants, and events of each day, just as water from a spring flows naturally with the bed of its watercourse.

As explained in my book *The God Catchers*:

> If you pursue His heart in passionate hunger, your words of desperation have the power to capture and "corner" His heart. In that moment, the Pursued becomes the Pursuer and the God Chaser becomes the God Catcher. . . .
>
> Our problem in the church is that if we are not careful, the arrogance of our spiritual adolescence robs us of our childlike passion for His presence. More than anything else, we must learn that *God does not hide so that He* cannot *be found; He is very careful to hide so that He* can *be found.*[1]

OUR APPROACH MAY CHANGE, BUT THE OBJECT OF OUR PURSUIT IS THE SAME

The pursuit of God's presence may take you through every conceivable situation life has to offer. Along the journey you may approach Him through prayers of desperation, but it is certain you will seek Him through prayers of repentance. The pursuit of Deity often begins with prayers of a hungry heart and moves on with prayers for wisdom and guidance.

As our hearts become more and more conformed to the heart of Jesus Christ, we find ourselves approaching Him with prayers of intercession for others. Things become especially exciting when we find the grace and courage to pray prayers of total surrender to God. In those times when His manifest presence engulfs us, He often begins to pray prayers of inspired faith and divine declaration *through* us; at other times we approach Him with prayers of struggle.

The prayers I suspect God longs for the most are those rare prayers of adoration we offer Him in our most godward moments. These nuggets of prayer arise when our thoughts are consumed by His beauty, and our personal needs and failures are forgotten for a few precious moments in the glory and warmth of His presence.

We probably need to spend a good part of our prayer time offering Him prayers of emptying—much as the bilge pumps of an ocean liner or oil tanker run constantly to pump out unwanted and unneeded waste prod-

> The prayers I suspect God longs for the most are those rare prayers of adoration we offer Him in our most godward moments.

ucts from the deep interior compartments—and we refill those empty spaces with fresh prayers of commitment to Him.

IMAGINE LIFE WITHOUT PRAYER

All of this speaks of "praying without ceasing" and prayer as natural and frequent as breathing itself. Now imagine life *without prayer.* (It marks the front porch of hell's domain in my thinking.) Subtract those moments of divine visitation and comfort. Temporarily forget those moments of healing you received in a thirty-second encounter with God's manifest presence—they would not have come without prayer.

I wrote *Prayers of a God Chaser* hoping most readers would understand that if you do *not* pray, you are not a God Chaser. If you *are* a God Chaser, then you *do* pray.

We have read, "He who comes to God must believe that He is, and that He is a rewarder of those who diligently seek Him."[2] If we hope to receive the reward of His manifest presence, we must be prepared to *diligently seek Him* in faith. Again, that takes us back to our knees, to our faces, to our prayer closets, to our altars, and to worship in all of its forms.

To be a Christian is to follow Christ. To follow Christ is to believe and do His Word, and to *pray.* I can't help but think of Andrew Murray's anointed assessment of prayer in a chapter entitled "The Sin of Prayerlessness" in *The Prayer Life*:

What is the reason that many thousands of Christian workers in the world do not have a greater influence? Nothing except this—the prayerlessness of their service. In the midst of all their zeal in the study and in the work of the Church, of all their faithfulness in preaching and conversation with the people, they lack that ceaseless prayer which has attached to it the sure promise of the Spirit and the power from on high. It is nothing but the sin of prayerlessness which is the cause of the lack of powerful spiritual life![3]

You and I are called to follow Jesus just as surely as were Peter, James, John, and the other nine disciples. They were at the head of the line, and you and I are not—that is the only difference that matters. God still intends to conform us to His image in the way we live, the way we pray, the way we serve, the way we deal with others, and in the way we die.

IF WE DO NOTHING ELSE, WE SHOULD PRAY

If Jesus did nothing else during His stay on earth, He *prayed*. His intimate relationship with the Father was marked, delineated, and flowed directly from His prayer life. That means that if you and I do nothing else during our stay on this earth, we should pray and worship Him.

In truth, we should do *everything* He asks us to do in this life. That includes at a minimum the careful and consistent study of His Word, faithful fellowship with other believers in a local church body, and the making of disciples. Yet it is all energized, organized, and authorized with power through the discipline and joy of fervent and effectual prayer.

What now? Pray. Seek Him, bless Him, love Him, follow Him, serve

Him from your knees until He asks you to do a deed. The Scriptures say, "Let everything that has breath praise the Lord."[4] For God Chasers with an addiction for His presence, that means pray without ceasing in the same way that you live and breathe without ceasing. The breaths of a God Chaser are synonymous with prayers and praise. We live for Him, we long for Him, we pant for Him. In short, we pray.

Lord, guide us in our pursuit, strengthen us in our chase, weaken us that we may lean upon You more; break us that we may feel Your hands remaking us once again.

Every day and in every way, allow us to draw closer to You as we pursue You with our words and the passion of our hearts. We will seek You early while You may be found. Answer us when we call—the more we find You, the more we long for You.

NOTES

CHAPTER 1

1. Leonard Ravenhill, *Why Revival Tarries* (Bloomington, Minn.: Bethany House Publishers, 1959), 17–18.
2. Richard J. Foster, *Prayer: Finding the Heart's True Home* (San Francisco: Harper-SanFrancisco, a division of HarperCollins Publishers, 1992).
3. Jesus' teaching on prayer, often called "The Lord's Prayer," appears in Matthew 6:9–13 and Luke 11:2–4.
4. Luke 18:10.
5. Luke 18:11a.
6. For more information on the negative role played by self-appointed passion police in our churches, see chapter 3, "No P.D.A.—Passion Police on Patrol" in my book *God's Eye View* (Nashville, Tenn.: Thomas Nelson, Inc., 2002).
7. I'm referring to the Lord's command in Revelation 2:4 that we return to our *first love.*
8. Ben Patterson, *Deepening Your Conversation With God: Learning to Love to Pray* (Minneapolis, Minn.: Bethany House Publishers, 2001), 18.
9. Paul describes the nature and effectiveness of our mighty weapons of warfare in 2 Corinthians 10:3–6 and Ephesians 6:10–18.
10. Jesus made it clear that He came to destroy the works of the Devil. That privilege and authority has been passed on to us (see 1 John 3:8).

CHAPTER 2

1. John 19:30.
2. Tommy Tenney, *The God Chasers* (Shippensburg, Pa.: Destiny Image Publishers, Inc., 1998), 2.
3. I have to believe He had a small foretaste when He gave up unbroken communion with His Father in the heavenly realm and humbled himself to invade our world in the frame of a tiny human baby (see Philippians 2:5–9).
4. E. M. Bounds, compiled by Leonard Ravenhill, *A Treasury of Prayer: The Best of*

E. M. Bounds on Prayer in a Single Volume (Minneapolis, Minn.: Bethany House Publishers, 1989), 24 (emphasis mine). E. M. Bounds went to be with the Lord in 1913, but the passionate writings of this man, who was one of the nation's greatest and most prolific prayer warriors since the American Civil War, continue to ignite holy fire in human hearts today.

5. A noted Bible scholar from the previous century, John E. McFadyen, said this about the value of prayers prayed in the past while discussing The Lord's Prayer in his book *The Prayers of the Bible* (Chattanooga, Tenn.: AMG Publishers, 1995), 172: "It must be borne in mind that even the Lord's prayer is a consecration of the past. It is original in the noblest sense of the word, but most of its individual petitions can be paralleled more or less closely from the Old Testament and other Jewish prayers. It is fresh and spontaneous—nothing could be more so—but *it does not sweep haughtily aside the prayers of the past.* It recognizes their abiding value by the way in which it uses them. It at once legitimizes and transforms them" (emphasis mine). This statement helps explain why I felt it helpful to include the prayers of Christian leaders from the past as well as biblical prayers in this book.

6. 1 Samuel 1:10–11.

7. Ben Patterson, *Deepening Your Conversation With God*, 125, citing a quotation of C. S. Lewis reproduced by Edythe Draper in *Draper's Book of Quotations for the Christian World* (Wheaton, Ill.: Tyndale House Publishers, 1992), No. 8257.

8. Tommy Tenney, *God's Favorite House: If You Build It, He Will Come* (Shippensburg, Pa.: Fresh Bread, an imprint of Destiny Image Publishers, Inc., 1999), 124–25.

9. E. M. Bounds, *Guide to Spiritual Warfare* (New Kensington, Pa.: Whitaker House, 1984), 151.

10. Condensed and adapted from a list of guidelines appearing in chapter 2 of John Maxwell, *Partners in Prayer: Support and Strengthen Your Pastor and Church Leaders* (Nashville, Tenn.: Thomas Nelson, Inc., 1996), 16–28.

11. Mark 10:47b.

12. E. M. Bounds, *A Treasury of Prayer*, 84.

13. St. Chrysostom, *The Works of Chrysostom, Homily XXXIV*. From Philip Schaff, ed., *A Select Library of the Nicene and Post-Nicene Fathers of the Christian Church* (Grand Rapids, Mich.: William B. Eerdman Publishing Company, n.d.), emphasis mine.

14. Tommy Tenney, *Experiencing His Presence: Devotions for God Catchers* (Nashville, Tenn.: Thomas Nelson Publishers, Inc., 2001), 131. This prayer appears at the end of the devotional article entitled "The Hungry Get Desperate, the Satisfied Become Apathetic" located on the third day of the seventh week in this twelve-week devotional book. It was written to accompany the book *The God Catchers*.

CHAPTER 3

1. The whole story appears in 2 Samuel 11–12.
2. Acts 13:22b–23.
3. Tommy Tenney, *The God Chasers*, 58.

4. Ibid., 60, insertion mine.
5. 1 Corinthians 1:29.
6. Jesus set a high standard for forgiveness and the avoidance of self-righteous judgments and condemnation of others in Luke 6:37.
7. Patrick D. Miller, *They Cried to the Lord: The Form and Theology of Biblical Prayer* (Minneapolis, Minn.: Fortress Press, 1994), 245 (emphasis mine).
8. Tommy Tenney, *The God Chasers*, 57.
9. Ibid., 60 (emphasis mine).
10. 2 Corinthians 7:9–11, emphasis mine.
11. See Luke 18:9–14.
12. 1 Peter 1:15–16, emphasis mine.
13. In John 14:26, Jesus told His disciples, "But the Helper, the Holy Spirit, whom the Father will send in My name, He will teach you all things, and bring to your remembrance all things that I said to you."
14. Philippians 2:13.
15. Veronica Zundel, compiler, *Eerdman's Book of Famous Prayers: A Treasury of Christian Prayers Through the Centuries* (Grand Rapids, Mich.: William B. Eerdman Publishing Company, 1983), 62.

CHAPTER 4

1. Acts 15:16–17, emphasis mine.
2. Psalm 34:8a.
3. This prayer appears at the beginning of an article written by Dale Evans Rogers entitled "Say Yes to God's Gift of Prayer." In Dale Salwak, ed., *The Power of Prayer* (New York: MJF Books, 1998), 47.
4. Tommy Tenney, *God's Favorite House*, 9–10 (bracketed insertions mine).
5. Ben Patterson, *Deepening Your Conversation With God*, 171.
6. Exodus 33:18–20, italics mine.
7. Tommy Tenney, *The God Chasers*, 139–40.
8. Luke 7:36–38.
9. Tommy Tenney, *The God Chasers*, 126.
10. From an article written by Yitzhak Buxbaum entitled "Praying for Real: Hasidic Teachings." In Dale Salwak, ed., *The Power of Prayer*, 186–87.
11. Julie K. Hogan, ed., *Ideals Treasury of Prayer* (Nashville, Tenn.: Ideals Publications, Inc., 2000), 136.
12. From an article written by Mother Teresa entitled "On Prayer." In Dale Salwak, ed., *The Power of Prayer*, 3–4 (emphasis mine).
13. "Hungry for You," chorus by Greg Johnson/Fire to the World Music; Verse by Jeannie Tenney/GodChaser Publishing. This song appears on two albums, "Holy Hunger" and "Passionate Pursuit," available directly through GodChasers.network and distributed nationally by Fresh Bread, an imprint of Destiny Image Publishers.

CHAPTER 5

1. 2 Chronicles 20:3–4.
2. 2 Chronicles 20:12b–13, emphasis mine.
3. 2 Chronicles 20:15–17a, NIV, emphasis mine.
4. 1 Peter 5:7, emphasis mine.
5. Genesis 24:12–16, emphasis mine.
6. A prayer by Frank MacNutt. In Julie K. Hogan, ed., *The Ideals Treasury of Prayer*, 96.
7. 2 Kings 19:14–16, 19, emphasis mine.
8. 2 Kings 19:20b.
9. See 2 Kings 19 for the whole story.
10. See 2 Samuel 5:17–21.
11. See 2 Samuel 5:22–25.
12. Richard J. Foster, *Prayer: Finding the Heart's True Home*, xii (emphasis mine).
13. It was at a Moravian meeting in London that John Wesley felt his heart "strangely warmed" and experienced a life-changing encounter with the Lord. He and his brother Charles later imparted that same holy passion to Great Britain and the American colonies and helped to ignite the First Great Awakening.
14. A prayer by Nicholas L. von Zinzendorf entitled "Jesus, Lead the Way." In Julie Hogan, ed., *The Ideals Treasury of Prayer*, 123.

CHAPTER 6

1. Matthew 5:44 NIV reads, "But I tell you: Love your enemies and pray for those who persecute you."
2. Romans 8:34.
3. Genesis 20:17–18 (note that I made key insertions to add clarity in this brief Scripture quote).
4. Numbers 21:7, emphasis mine.
5. Deuteronomy 9:18–20, emphasis mine.
6. 2 Kings 4:32–36, emphasis mine.
7. Job 42:10, emphasis mine.
8. Daniel 9:3, 16–17, 19.
9. Ephesians 3:14–21.
10. Luke 22:31–32.
11. John 17:11, 20–21.
12. Quoted by John C. Maxwell, *Partners in Prayer: Support and Strengthen Your Pastor and Church Leaders*, 7.
13. Ibid., 10.
14. See 1 Thessalonians 5:17.
15. Romans 8:26–27, emphasis mine.
16. Watchman Nee, *Let Us Pray* [Translated from the Chinese] (New York: Christian Fellowship Publishers, Inc., 1977), 34–35, emphasis mine.

17. Lillian Herlands Hornstein, G. D. Percy, Calvin S. Brown, eds., *The Reader's Companion to World Literature*, 2nd edition (New York: A Mentor Book, New American Library, 1973), 520.
18. Julie K. Hogan, ed., *Ideals Treasury of Prayer*, 103.

CHAPTER 7

1. Veronica Zundel, compiler, *Eerdman's Book of Famous Prayers: A Treasury of Christian Prayers Through the Centuries*, 88.
2. Luke 9:23–24.
3. 1 John 4:18b.
4. Richard Foster, *Prayer: Finding the Heart's True Home*, 3 (emphasis mine).
5. Isaiah 6:8b.
6. See Isaiah 20:3.
7. Elmer Towns and Douglas Porter, *The Ten Greatest Revivals Ever: From Pentecost to the Present* (Ann Arbor, Mich.: Vine Books, an imprint of Servant Publications, 2000), 29.
8. 1 Corinthians 6:20, emphasis mine.
9. Romans 12:1, emphasis mine.
10. Ralph Waldo Emerson, "On Our Faces" (emphasis mine). In Constance Pollock and Daniel Pollock, *The Book of Uncommon Prayer* (Dallas, Tex.: Word Publishing, 1996), 61.
11. Dale Salwak, ed., *The Power of Prayer*, xii-xiii (emphasis mine).
12. Veronica Zundel, compiler, *Eerdman's Book of Famous Prayers*, 81.

CHAPTER 8

1. Ben Patterson, *Deepening Your Conversation With God*, 12 (emphasis mine).
2. 1 Peter 4:10–11, emphasis mine.
3. Acts 3:6–7 KJV, emphasis mine.
4. Acts 4:29–31, emphasis mine.
5. This is a reference to the statement by John the Baptist, "He must increase, but I must decrease" (John 3:30).
6. Ronnie W. Floyd, *How to Pray: Developing an Intimate Relationship With God* (Nashville, Tenn.: Word Publishing, a division of Thomas Nelson Company, 1999), 148–49 (emphasis mine).
7. Ibid., 149–50.
8. A. W. Pink, Donald R. White, ed., *Effectual Fervent Prayer* (Grand Rapids, Mich.: Baker Book House, 1981), 221. The Scripture passage cited by the author is Revelation 1:5b–6 KJV.
9. E. M. Bounds, *The Weapon of Prayer* (Grand Rapids, Mich.: Baker Book House, 1991), 26–27 (emphasis mine).
10. Richard J. Foster, and James Bryan Smith, ed., *Devotional Classics: Selected Readings*

for Individuals and Groups, Letter 227 (San Francisco: HarperSanFrancisco, a division of HarperCollins Publishers, 1993), 220 (emphasis mine).
11. Ibid., 223.
12. Ephesians 3:14–21, emphasis mine.
13. See 1 Kings 18:19.
14. 1 Kings 18:36b–39, emphasis mine.
15. Read of their powerful ministry in Trevor Yaxley, *William and Catherine: A New Biography* (Bethany House Publishers, 2002).
16. Correspondence between John Wesley and a friend. In E. M. Bounds, *The Weapon of Prayer*, 114.

CHAPTER 9
1. See the distraught father's description of the way his epileptic son suffered in Matthew 17:15b.
2. Mark 9:24.
3. See Mark 9:22–24.
4. Matthew 8:1–3, emphasis mine.
5. Tommy Tenney, *God's Favorite House*, 80–81.
6. Ibid.
7. Job 13:13–15a, emphasis mine.
8. Tommy Tenney, *The God Catchers: Experiencing the Manifest Presence of God* (Nashville, Tenn.: Thomas Nelson, Inc., 2000).
9. Julie K. Hogan, ed., *Ideals Treasury of Prayer*, 26.
10. Ibid., 114.
11. Psalm 73:25–26.
12. Veronica Zundel, compiler, *Eerdman's Book of Famous Prayers*, 78.

CHAPTER 10
1. *Merriam-Webster's Collegiate Dictionary*, 10th edition (Springfield, Mo.: Merriam-Webster, Inc., 1994), 16.
2. Richard J. Foster, *Prayer: Finding the Heart's True Home*, 81.
3. See Ephesians 5.
4. Tommy Tenney, *Chasing God, Serving Man: Divine Encounters Between Martha's Kitchen and Mary's Worship* (Shippensburg, Pa.: Fresh Bread, an imprint of Destiny Image Publishers, Inc., 2001), 162, emphasis mine.
5. Tommy Tenney, *God's Favorite House*, 82.
6. John refers to his habit of laying his head on the Lord's chest twice in his own gospel (see John 13:25; 21:20).
7. Jesus gave the nickname "Sons of Thunder" to James and John in Mark 3:17b.
8. Song of Songs 1:1–3 NIV.
9. In Revelation 2:4, the Lord *commands* us to return to Him as our first love. Perhaps

we should extend this same command to our strongest earthly commitment as well—our loving Father always empowers us to obey those things He commands!

10. Richard J. Foster, *Prayer: Finding the Heart's True Home*, 82–83.

11. Bartimaeus was perhaps the church's first "parade crasher" because desperation drove him to crash and disrupt the "Jesus parade" as it passed through Jericho. If you are hungry for more, see Mark 10:46–52. Then you may want to turn to chapter 5, "When Destiny Meets Desperation," in *The God Catchers*, 61–73.

12. Richard J. Foster, *Prayer: Finding the Heart's True Home*, 87.

13. Luke 7:37–38.

14. Dig deeper into God's unparalleled response to the miracle of this woman's "alabaster-box-breaking passion" in chapter 9, "Dismantle Your Glory," Tommy Tenney, *The God Chasers*.

15. Tommy Tenney, *The God Chasers*, 126.

16. Tommy Tenney, *God's Eye View*, 59.

17. Tommy Tenney, *Chasing God, Serving Man*, 163.

18. This prayer is one of my favorite selections from my twelve-week devotional book, *Experiencing His Presence: Devotions for God Catchers*, 199.

CHAPTER 11

1. T. F. Tenney and Tommy Tenney, *Secret Sources of Power: Rediscovering Biblical Power Points* (Shippensburg, Pa.: Fresh Bread, an imprint of Destiny Image Publishers, Inc., 2000), 115.

2. 1 Peter 5:8b.

3. Satan, the chief of demons, is also called Beelzebub in many places in the Bible, including Luke 11:15–22. It means "dung-king" or "lord of the flies" according to James Strong, *Strong's Exhaustive Concordance of the Bible* (Peabody, Mass.: Hendrickson Publishers, n.d.), Greek #954 and Hebrew #1176, respectively.

4. Galatians 2:20a, emphasis mine.

5. Luke 11:24–26, emphasis mine.

6. This is a reference to the Scripture passages that declare: "Therefore, if anyone is in Christ, *he is a new creation; old things have passed away*; behold, all things have become new" (2 Corinthians 5:17, emphasis mine); and "Do not lie to one another, since you have *put off the old man with his deeds*, and have *put on the new man* who is *renewed in knowledge* according to the image of Him who created him" (Colossians 3:9–10, emphasis mine).

7. Tenney & Tenney, *Secret Sources of Power*, 116.

8. 2 Corinthians 12:7–8, emphasis mine.

9. Tenney & Tenney, *Secret Sources of Power*, 122.

10. Julie Hogan, ed., *Ideals Treasury of Prayer*, 46.

11. See Exodus 4:1–4.

12. See Exodus 7:10–12. *Note:* No one really knows how many magicians were involved in the confrontation, but the two brothers who led them (and were the chief recipi-

ents of God's scorn) are identified in rabbinic tradition and in 2 Timothy 3:8 as Jannes and Jambres.

13. For more about the value and virtue of emptiness in God's economy, see chapter 7, "Collected Emptiness" in *The God Catchers*, 97–112.
14. Tenney & Tenney, *Secret Sources of Power*, 133.
15. Julie Hogan, ed., *Ideals Treasury of Prayer*, 46.
16. Luke 9:23, emphasis mine.
17. John 3:3, emphasis mine.
18. See Matthew 28:1–10 for one of the most exciting Bible passages of all times, and remember *that* is the power Christ released in *your life* the day you said "yes."
19. Veronica Zundel, compiler, *Eerdman's Book of Famous Prayers: A Treasury of Christian Prayers Through the Centuries*, 39.

CHAPTER 12
1. Luke 23:46b.
2. See Matthew 12:36–37.
3. Ruth 1:16–17.
4. This story appears in greater detail in the book I co-wrote with David Cape entitled *God's Secret to Greatness: The Power of the Towel* (Ventura, Calif.: Regal Books, a division of Gospel Light, 2000), 166.
5. Joshua 24:14–15, emphasis mine.
6. Richard J. Foster, *Prayer: Finding the Heart's True Home*, 67.
7. Job 13:15a. *Note:* A fuller form of this passage was quoted earlier in chapter 9, "Prayers of Struggle." Job's remarkable prayer justifies double mention for its purity under fire and power in the midst of adversity.
8. This is my supposition from the first seven verses of 1 Samuel 1. Hannah didn't "suddenly" acquire the power or ability to pray in one day. The words of her recorded prayers tell us she was well versed in prayer and even in the Scriptures (see 1 Samuel 1:11; 2:1–10).
9. Veronica Zundel, compiler, *Eerdman's Book of Famous Prayers: A Treasury of Christian Prayers Through the Centuries*, 44.
10. Andrew Murray, *The Prayer Life* (Springdale, Pa.: Whitaker House, 1981), 88–89. (Soon to be released by Bethany House under the title *Living the Prayerful Life*, newly edited for today's reader.)
11. See Philippians 4:13.
12. Philippians 2:12–16, emphasis mine.
13. See 1 Corinthians 15:55–57.

EPILOGUE
1. Tommy Tenney, *The God Catchers*, 12.
2. Hebrews 11:6b.
3. Andrew Murray, *The Prayer Life*, 15.
4. Psalm 150:6.

BIBLIOGRAPHY

Appleton, George. General editor. *The Oxford Book of Prayer*. New York: Oxford University Press, 1985.

Bounds, E. M. *Guide to Spiritual Warfare*. New Kensington, Pa.: Whitaker House, 1984. *Note:* This book was formerly titled *Winning the Invisible War*, and was originally titled *Satan: His Personality, Power, and Overthrow*.

———. *The Necessity of Prayer*. Grand Rapids, Mich.: Baker Books, a division of Baker Book House Company, 1991.

———. *The Possibilities of Prayer*. Grand Rapids, Mich.: Baker Books, a division of Baker Book House Company, 1991.

———. *The Weapon of Prayer*. Grand Rapids, Mich.: Baker Books, a division of Baker Book House Company, 1991.

———. Leonard Ravenhill, compiler. *A Treasury of Prayer: The Best of E. M. Bounds on Prayer in a Single Volume*. Minneapolis, Minn.: Bethany House Publishers, 1989.

Chrysostom, St. *The Works of Chrysostom, Homily* XXXIV. From Philip Schaff, ed. *A Select Library of the Nicene and Post-Nicene Fathers of the Christian Church*. Grand Rapids, Mich.: William B. Eerdman Publishing Company, n.d.

Copeland, Germaine. *Prayers That Avail Much*. Commemorative gift edition. Tulsa, Okla.: Harrison House, Inc., 1997.

Draper, Edythe. *Draper's Book of Quotations for the Christian World*. Wheaton, Ill.: Tyndale House Publishers, 1992.

Floyd, Ronnie W. *How to Pray: Developing an Intimate Relationship With God*. Nashville, Tenn.: Word Publishing, a Thomas Nelson Company, 1999.

Foster, Richard J. *Prayer: Finding the Heart's True Home*. San Francisco: HarperSanFrancisco, a division of HarperCollins Publishers, 1992.

Foster, Richard J., and James Bryan Smith, ed. *Devotional Classics: Selected Readings for Individuals and Groups.* San Francisco: HarperSanFrancisco, a division of HarperCollins Publishers, 1993.

Hannegraaff, Hank. *The Prayer of Jesus: Secrets to Real Intimacy With God.* Nashville, Tenn.: Word Publishing, a Thomas Nelson Company, 2001.

Hogan, Julie K., ed., *Ideals Treasury of Prayer.* Nashville, Tenn.: Ideals Publications, Inc., 2000.

Hornstein, Lillian Herlands, G. D. Percy, Calvin S. Brown, eds. *The Reader's Companion to World Literature,* 2nd edition. New York: A Mentor Book, New American Library, 1973.

Leman, Dr. Kevin. *Keeping Your Family Together When the World Is Falling Apart.* New York: Delacorte Press, Bantam Doubleday Dell Publishing Group, Inc., 1992.

Lockyer, Herbert. *All the Prayers of the Bible.* Grand Rapids, Mich.: Zondervan Publishing Co., 1959.

Lucado, Max, with Jenna, Andrea & Sara Lucado. Illustrations by Liz Bonham. *The Crippled Lamb.* Nashville, Tenn.: Tommy Nelson, a division of Thomas Nelson, Inc., 1999.

Maxwell, John. *Partners in Prayer: Support and Strengthen Your Pastor and Church Leaders.* Nashville, Tenn.: Thomas Nelson, Inc., 1996.

McFadyen, John E. *The Prayers of the Bible.* Chattanooga, Tenn.: AMG Publishers, 1995.

Miller, Patrick D. *They Cried to the Lord: The Form and Theology of Biblical Prayer.* Minneapolis, Minn.: Fortress Press, 1994.

Nee, Watchman. *Let Us Pray.* Translated from the Chinese. New York: Christian Fellowship Publishers, Inc., 1977.

Omartian, Stormie. *The Power of a Praying Husband.* Eugene, Ore.: Harvest House Publishers, 2001.

———. *The Power of a Praying Wife.* Eugene, Ore.: Harvest House Publishers, 1997.

———. *Praying God's Will for Your Life: A Prayerful Walk to Spiritual Well-Being.* Nashville, Tenn.: Thomas Nelson Publishers, a division of Thomas Nelson, Inc., 2001.

Patterson, Ben. *Deepening Your Conversation With God: Learning to Love to Pray.* Minneapolis, Minn.: Bethany House Publishers, 2001.

Pink, A. W., and Donald R. White, ed. *Effectual Fervent Prayer.* Grand Rapids, Mich.: Baker Book House, 1981.

Pollock, Constance, and Daniel Pollock. *The Book of Uncommon Prayer.* Dallas, Tex.: Word Publishing, 1996.

Ravenhill, Leonard. *Why Revival Tarries.* Bloomington, Minn.: Bethany House Publishers, 1959 (still in print).

Salwak, Dale, ed. *The Power of Prayer.* New York: MJF Books, 1998.

Schaff, Philip, ed. *A Select Library of the Nicene and Post-Nicene Fathers of the Christian Church.* Grand Rapids, Mich.: William B. Eerdman Publishing Company, n.d.

Strong, James. *Strong's Exhaustive Concordance of the Bible.* Peabody, Mass.: Hendrickson Publishers, n.d.

Tenney, T. F., and Tommy Tenney. *Secret Sources of Power: Rediscovering Biblical Power Points.* Shippensburg, Pa.: Fresh Bread, an imprint of Destiny Image Publishers, Inc., 2000.

Tenney, Tommy. *Chasing God, Serving Man: Divine Encounters Between Martha's Kitchen and Mary's Worship.* Shippensburg, Pa.: Fresh Bread, an imprint of Destiny Image Publishers, Inc., 2001.

———. *Experiencing His Presence: Devotions for God Catchers.* Nashville, Tenn.: Thomas Nelson Publishers, Inc., 2001.

———. *The God Catchers: Experiencing the Manifest Presence of God.* Nashville, Tenn.: Thomas Nelson, Inc., 2000.

———. *The God Chasers.* Shippensburg, Pa.: Destiny Image Publishers, Inc., 1998.

———. *God's Eye View.* Nashville, Tenn.: Thomas Nelson, Inc., 2002.

———. *God's Favorite House: If You Build It, He Will Come.* Shippensburg, Pa.: Fresh Bread, an imprint of Destiny Image Publishers, Inc., 1999.

Towns, Elmer, and Douglas Porter. *The Ten Greatest Revivals Ever: From Pentecost to the Present.* Ann Arbor, Mich.: Vine Books, an imprint of Servant Publications, 2000.

Wilkinson, Bruce. *The Prayer of Jabez: Breaking Through to the Blessed Life.* Sisters, Ore.: Multnomah Publishers, Inc., 2000.

Yaxley, Trevor. *William and Catherine: A New Biography.* Bethany House Publishers, 2002.

Zundel, Veronica, compiler. *Eerdman's Book of Famous Prayers: A Treasury of Christian Prayers Through the Centuries.* Grand Rapids, Mich.: William B. Eerdman Publishing Company, 1983.

GodChasers.network is the ministry of Tommy and Jeannie Tenney. Their heart's desire is to see the presence and power of God fall—not just in churches, but on cities and communities all over the world.

How to contact us:

By Mail:

GodChasers.network
P.O. Box 3355
Pineville, Louisiana 71361
USA

By Phone:

Voice:	318.44CHASE (318.442.4273)
Fax:	318.442.6884
Orders:	888.433.3355

By Internet:

E-mail:	GodChaser@GodChasers.net
Website:	www.GodChasers.net

BOOKS BY

Tony Teny

THE GOD CHASERS
$12.00 plus $4.50 S&H

What is a God Chaser? A person whose hunger exceeds his reach…a person whose passion for God's presence presses him to chase the impossible in hopes that the uncatchable might catch him.

The great GodChasers of the Scripture—Moses, Daniel, David—see how they were driven by hunger born of tasting His goodness. They had seen the invisible and nothing else satisfied. Add your name to the list. Come join the ranks of the God Chasers.

GOD'S EYE VIEW
$23.00 plus $4.50 S&H

In this simple but powerful book, worship will teach you "throne zone" secrets. The higher you go in worship, the bigger God appears (and the smaller your problems seem). If you can't see that from where you are presently sitting, there is a better seat available. The angels will usher you to your reserved seat in "heavenly places" and you will have *God's Eye View.*

CHASING GOD, SERVING MAN
$17.00 plus $4.50 S&H

Using the backdrop of Bethany and the house of Mary and Martha, Tommy Tenney biblically explores new territory. The revolutionary concepts in this book can change your life. You will discover who you really are (and unlock the secret of who "they" really are)!

MARY'S PRAYERS & MARTHA'S RECIPES
$18.00 plus $4.50 S&H

There are a lot of prayer books and many great spiritual books but there are precious few prayer and compassion books that are practical workbooks as well. *Mary's Prayers and Martha's Recipes* will be your own special resource for both seasons in your life.

We must learn to work like Martha and worship like Mary. It is essential that we do not do one to the exclusion of the other. It takes the loving service of Martha and the adoring prayers of Mary to complete the full ministry of the Body of Christ in this world.

GodChasers.network
P.O. Box 3355, Pineville, Louisiana 71361-3355
318-44CHASE (318.442.4273)
www.GodChasers.net

Run With Us!

Become a GodChasers.network Monthly Revival Partner

GodChasers are people whose hunger for Him compels them to run—not walk—towards a deeper and more meaningful relationship with the Almighty! For them, it isn't just a casual pursuit. Traditional Sundays and Wednesdays aren't enough—they need Him everyday, in every situation and circumstance, the good times and bad. Are you a GodChaser? Do you believe the body of Christ needs Revival? If my mandate of personal, National and International Revival is a message that resonates in your spirit, I want you to prayfully consider Running with us! Our Revival Partners fuel GodChasers.network to bring the message of unity and the pursuit of His presence around the world! And the results are incredible, yet humbling. As a Revival Partner, your monthly seed becomes the matches we use to set Revival fires around the globe.

For your monthly support of at least thirty dollars or more, I will send you free, personal fuel each month. This could be audio or videotapes of what I feel the Lord is saying that month. In addition, you will receive discounts on all of our ministry resources. Your Revival Partner status will automatically include you in invitation-only gatherings where I will minister in a more intimate setting.

I rely on our Revival Partners to intercede for the ministry in prayer and even minister with us at GodChaser gatherings around the country. I love to sow seed in peoples' lives and have learned that you can't out give God, He always multiplies the seed! If we give Him something to work with, there's no limit how many He can feed, or how many Revival fires can be started!

Will you run with us every month?

In Pursuit,

Tommy Tenney

Become a Monthly Revival Partner by calling or writing to:

Tommy Tenney/GodChasers.network
P.O. Box 3355, Pineville, Louisiana 71361-3355
318.44CHASE (318.442.4273)